who knew?™

the MONEY DIET

FOUR WEEKS TO YOUR FINANCIAL FITNESS

- 1,000s OF PROVEN TIPS • SIMPLE SAVING SECRETS
- EASY STRATEGIES TO ELIMINATE DEBT

BRUCE LUBIN & JEANNE BOSSOLINA-LUBIN

© 2013 Castle Point Publishing, LLC

Castle Point Publishing
58 Ninth Street
Hoboken, NJ 07030

We've calculated the savings amounts in *The Money Diet* based on average expenses for a family of four, and in many cases, showed you how much you will save over the course of a year. Prices may fluctuate and vary geographically, so these savings amounts are meant to be a guide only. You may save more or less depending on where you live. And if you do, please write to us at www.whoknewtips.com so we can incorporate your experiences in future editions of this book!

Cover design by Michele L. Trombley

ISBN: 978-0-9883264-6-0

Printed and bound in the United States of America

2 4 6 8 10 9 7 5 4 3 1

Please visit us online at www.WhoKnewTips.com

DEDICATION

To Holly Schmidt, Aimee Chase, and Michele Trombley, for their indispensible help, unparalleled work ethic, and more than anything, for being such extraordinary friends.

ACKNOWLEDGEMENTS

The Money Diet was born during Hurricane Sandy, in flooded, blacked-out Hoboken, New Jersey, and simply could not have been created without the dedication of a wonderful group of generous people. While Jeanne and I dealt with our beloved hometown and the immediate needs of so many neighbors, Heather Rodino, Devorah Lev-Tov, Lindsay Herman, Amy Kover, Jenifer Scott, and Ron Dicker all pitched in and delivered amazing work at breakneck speed. Our talented longtime friend, Sue Livingston, pushed this book over the finish line, which made us love her even more, if that's possible. Our printers, Melissa Grover and Todd Vanek, printed on time, which was nothing short of a miracle. Jennifer Boudinot helped with the original idea and research for *The Money Diet*, and we're thankful as always for her big brain. And we're especially grateful to the ladies of Ingenious Designs, who dealt with every setback with patience and understanding. Many thanks to all of you!

TABLE OF CONTENTS

INTRODUCTION

If you have ever been on a diet, you know that losing weight isn't an overnight phenomenon (even if we wish it were!). It comes from making lots of good decisions over time about little things—like whether or not to have one more chocolate cupcake. The same goes for your money! If you want to put your spending on a diet and keep more of your hard-earned dough, this book can help you control your usual spending urges and teach you to save in ways you never expected!

We developed this fun and easy 28-day Money Diet plan so you can start enjoying a richer, better life and rid yourself of some money stress. Each chapter addresses a major area of potential savings and represents a new day of your diet. Read in sequence or skip around (we know you can't wait to read the money-saving secrets in Chapter 12). You won't believe how many tips there are for saving $5 to $500 to $5,000 on everything from dog food to phone bills to college tuition and beyond. Tally up the savings totals in bold and start thinking about all the things you can do with that extra money!

In addition to thousands of trusty **Who Knew? Savings Tips**, we've built in some encouraging **Daily Inspirations** to help keep you positive and on track. The **Financial Fitness** section will guide you in handling your personal finances. Want to know how to organize your financial records for easy reference? Need some help improving your credit score or taking your first dip into the stock market? Each day of your diet will give you more wisdom and advice for making the most of your money.

Are you ready to get started? Read on and see for yourself how easy and exciting saving money can be. Anyone can master this Money Diet. It doesn't matter whether you've been successful at saving money in the past. Today you start fresh, knowing that the best financial shape of your life is just one month away!

Thriftily yours,
Jeanne and Bruce

P.S. You can eat as many chocolate cupcakes as you want on this diet—just be sure to buy the ingredients on sale.

DAY 1
SUPERMARKET SMARTS

DAILY INSPIRATION

With three boys in the house, we know how food costs can add up, so on Day 1 we'll get you started with our best tips and tricks for making the most of every food dollar. First you'll learn meal planning, and then we'll head out to the supermarket together to put that plan into action.

When was the last time you let yourself dream a bit about your goals? It's often hard to think ahead when you're trying to keep up with the stresses of everyday life. Today we'd like you to take it easy. Let yourself daydream about what you would do if you had more financial freedom—vacations, a new car, extra time with family, and the feeling of knowing that you're taking care of it all! If you don't have time to take a relaxing bath or to walk around the block, carve out a block of time during your commute or daily shower to dream big. Then write down those dreams—even if they're not related to money! Instead of feeling bad that you can't have everything you want right now, let it empower you to get there some day.

DAILY SAVINGS SUBJECT
Supermarket Smarts

WHO KNEW?   **QUICK TIP**

Save the boxes from name-brand cereal your kids are
attached to, then empty the generic products into them.
Your picky eaters won't know the difference if they can't see
it on the outside.

Savings amount: $390 a year on cereal.

KEY STRATEGY: PLAN YOUR MEALS

According to the USDA, the average American family of
four spends between $10,000–12,000 per year on food.
Your actual expenses might be somewhat higher or lower,
but the point is that a significant portion of your salary
is going toward food costs. While these figures may be
frightening, they're actually good news because it means
there's lots of room for savings! If you're going to save
money on food costs, you have to start planning your

meals. It's as simple as it sounds. Figure out what you're eating for dinner a week or two in advance and you'll waste less food because all of your ingredients will be accounted for. (No more tossing out impulse items that spoiled before you could figure out what to do with them.) To make life even easier, try to make several meals at one time, so you can freeze or refrigerate them for later. Here are some other tips to get you started on meal planning.

- **Begin with what you know.** Pick five to seven meals that your family loves and that you could make with your eyes closed. Try to include some that you can easily stretch to two meals—for example, a giant pot of soup or chili, a large casserole, or a big batch of pasta.

- **Write out your meals for the week.** You can use a white board or a Post-It note tacked to the wall. Include the meals that are made from leftovers and jot down when you plan to eat out. This will not only make you more motivated to follow through, but will hopefully get your family more involved.

- **Don't stray too far from your list of ingredients.** As meal planning becomes ingrained in your everyday routine, try to plan your meals around what's on sale at the grocery store or what you have on hand. You'll avoid impulse buys and waste less food.

- **Plan meals that use the same ingredient(s).** Plan a casserole on Monday and a stew on Wednesday and buy big bags of veggies to use in both. That way, you get the best price on your veggies and make cooking a little easier.
- **Save your weekly menu and use it again.** This will save you some thinking time and is especially handy when the meats you used one week are on sale again.

WHO KNEW? **QUICK TIP**

When you're at the supermarket, make sure you keep a close watch while your items are being rung up. A recent study found that 10 percent of items are scanned in at the incorrect price.

Potential savings amount: $1,200 a year.

MAXIMIZE SUPERMARKET SAVINGS

Now that you know how to plan your meals, let's hit the supermarket aisles. We've had *years* of experience in this area, so here are some of our all-time favorite money-saving suggestions.

- **Follow the golden rule of grocery shopping.** We know you've heard it before, but it bears repeating: never go to the grocery store on an empty stomach. If you're hungry, you'll not only want to rush through shopping (taking less time to compare unit prices), but you'll also make more impulse purchases because everything looks so tasty! Eat before you go and save money.

- **Switch to the store brand for super savings.** When you've been buying the same brand-name product for as long as you can remember, it's hard to make the switch to generics. However, you'll be surprised when you find that many generic and store-brand products taste exactly the same (or better!) for around 30 to 50 percent less. Always buy generic baking ingredients such as flour, oil, and sugar. They are indistinguishable from their more expensive counterparts. Frozen and canned vegetables are also usually exactly the same. As for products such as cereals, cookies, and crackers, basic is better—we've had good luck with plain granola, potato chips, and wheat crackers. No matter what the product, it never hurts to try. If you end up having to throw away one can of soup, you've wasted a few dollars, but if you like it, you can save a lot over the course of a year. The average household spends around $5,500 per year on name-brand groceries, so your savings could be huge. *ANNUAL SAVINGS: $1,650 OR MORE.*

- **Look down for savings.** When you're checking out prices at the store, take a look at the lowest shelf first and work your way up. You'll find that the highest prices are at eye level—since that's where people in a hurry will most likely grab a product from.

- **Weigh before you pay.** If you're buying produce that is priced by the item rather than by the pound (such as a head of lettuce, lemons, or avocados), take advantage of the store's scales and weigh them to find the heaviest one. The savings might be small, but you'll get more for your money.

- **Cut back on convenience.** Remember the cardinal rule when it comes to saving money on food: If it's "convenient," it's probably costly. For example, pickles cut flat for sandwiches, juice in single-serving bottles, pre-shredded cheese, and cubed butternut squash. One bag of pretzels, for example, costs you about $2 while the same amount in individual bags is $4 or more! Think carefully about what you're buying, look at the difference in price per ounce, and decide if the convenience is worth the extra cost! *SAVINGS AMOUNT: 50 PERCENT OR MORE PER ITEM.*

Buying yourself a prepaid grocery store gift card is a great way to stick to a food budget! Think of it as a portable checking account: Put money on the card, then "withdraw" from it every time you shop. With a dedicated grocery "account," you'll find it's easier to keep a tighter rein on your spending. If you normally exceed your grocery budget by 15 percent, you can save thousands.

Annual savings: $1,900.

- **Buy in bulk—ends, that is.** Ask at the deli counter of your supermarket if they offer a discount for "bulk ends." These end bits of sliced meats are too small to slice in the machine, but can be sliced or cubed at home. They're often offered at half off! If you spend $10 a week in cold cuts, the savings could really add up. *ANNUAL SAVINGS: $260.*

- **Take down the cost of takeout.** It's OK to get takeout for dinner every once in a while—especially if you use this great trick for keeping the costs down—but next time order from the lunch menu! We're sure you've noticed that many takeout joints offer lunch specials of similar portion for up to 30 percent less. Few of us can eat what the restaurant considers dinner-sized portions anyway. Buy in the afternoon, stash in the fridge, and then reheat at dinner for savings! If you spend $30–40 twice a week feeding a family of four, you could save around a thousand dollars a year. ***ANNUAL SAVINGS: $936–$1,248.***

- **Don't take the kids grocery shopping.** You've been there—the kids are screaming and begging you to buy a certain cereal or a particular flavor of chips. Your patience is shot and you give in, hoping it will make for a faster and less painful shopping trip. Did you know that taking kids to the supermarket adds an average of 10 percent to your grocery bill? With the typical family of four spending around $900–$1,000 a month on food, it can add up. ***ANNUAL SAVINGS: $1,080–$1,200.***

WHO KNEW?　　QUICK TIP

Stop the plastic water bottle habit. Bottled water is not only costly, but all of that plastic is bad for the environment. Switch to a filtered water system, like Brita or PUR, and save big.

Annual savings: $1,400.

WHO KNEW?   QUICK TIP

Nothing beats the convenience of pre-shredded cheese, but opting for a brick of cheddar or a ball of mozzarella will save you $2–$3 a pound.

Annual savings: $210.

- **Buy in bulk and split items with a friend.** We love to shop the big warehouse stores like Costco, BJ's, or Sam's Club. They can provide lots of great deals, but they're also full of budget booby-traps. You might go in looking for toilet paper, paper towels, and bulk meat, and end up walking out with a 20-pack of canned tuna, a brand-new GPS, and a pair of discounted designer jeans. What's more, some of the items come in such large quantities that it's impossible to use them all before they spoil, and you end up throwing, say, half of that five-pound box of grapes in the trash. Instead, go shopping with a friend or relative. That way, you can split the larger items and stay on budget, wasting a lot less food—and money. With an average purchase at Costco totaling around $110, you could save hundreds of dollars a year. *ANNUAL SAVINGS: $500 OR MORE.*

- **Not a member? No problem.** If you're not a member of a wholesale club, you can often still take advantage of the savings. Have a friend who is a member get you a gift card, and they'll let you shop there without a membership! (Just make sure to call the store and check first.) Show a gift card at the front desk and most wholesale clubs will let you in without a membership card. Many wholesale clubs have free 30-day trial memberships so look out for those in your mail. *ANNUAL SAVING: $50-$100 IN MEMBERSHIP COSTS, PLUS SAVINGS ON BUYING IN BULK!*

- **Shop beyond the supermarket.** When hunting for the best prices, don't let your journey stop at the supermarket. Sometimes stores that don't specialize in groceries will actually give you the lowest price staple items. CVS, Walgreens, and other drug stores are also good places to buy certain foods, such as soup, spaghetti sauce, and candy. Make sure to take a walk down these stores' food aisles and compare the prices to your regular supermarket, especially the food that's on sale. Another great place to find low prices on food is at your local dollar store.

- **Check out the newest store.** Any time a new grocery store opens up in our area, we always stop by to take a look. It may be a pain to navigate differently laid-out aisles, but new supermarkets offer big sales and the lowest prices possible in their first few weeks and months of business as an incentive to get shoppers to switch stores. Many stores also offer contests and giveaways to celebrate their grand openings, so visiting during the first week is a good idea.

- **Use your cell phone to save.** CompareMe Shopping Utility is a cell phone app that lets you compare unit prices of competitive store products in an instant. Ziplist and Grocery IQ can organize your shopping list by aisle when you tell it what store you shop at! Your cell phone can help you in so many ways!

WHO KNEW?   QUICK TIP

Brown and white eggs are nearly the same in terms of nutritional value. The only difference is that they are laid by different breeds of chickens. Brown eggs are usually more expensive because the breed of hen that lays them requires more food. The farmer passes that expense onto you. Buy white eggs and save 30 percent. ***Annual savings: $30.***

DAY 1
FINANCIAL FITNESS PLAN
Turning Your Dreams into Achievable Goals

Consider your dreams for the future. Which of those would you most like to make a reality? Pick the top two or three "must-dos." Make sure they're in sync with the other dreams you wrote about. Maybe you wrote that you wanted to buy a Porsche or a have an enviable collection of designer shoes (remember, we didn't impose any limits on this list!), but those ambitions might not mesh with a more important goal of spending more time with your family or saving for your child's education, for example. Once you've got your list narrowed down, follow these steps:

- **Assign a time frame to each dream.** How long will your dream take to become real? To start building confidence, give yourself some short-term goals in addition to the longer-term ones. In one month, I want to cut $100 from my grocery bill. In two years I'd like to have paid off my credit card. In five years, I'd like to have saved up enough money for a down payment on a house. In ten years, I want to have a sizable college fund for my toddler.

- **Start researching.** Now is the time when the dream starts to take shape. Begin by investigating what it takes to achieve the goal. Write a list of the specific steps required. What will it take to go from where you are now to where you want to be? How much money will it cost? Do you know anyone who has accomplished the same thing from whom you can ask for guidance? For example, if you're looking to save money for a down payment on a house, you might begin by looking at housing prices in your area and asking yourself how much you'd like to have saved toward a down payment. If your goal is 10 percent, calculate how much that is. For a home worth $200,000, you'd need $20,000. What can you do to get to your goal of saving $4,000 a year for five years? Broken down, that's $333 per month, or $83 per week.

- **Ask yourself what you are willing to do to achieve it.** Just by being on the Money Diet, you will be able to reduce expenses in almost every area of your life. But would you also be willing to take an extra shift or two this month to shave a year off that student loan? Could you put up with having a roommate if it meant cutting your rent in half?

- **Start acting.** You know the old saying: a journey of a thousand miles starts with a single step. In this case, it's true. Keep the goal in sight, but don't let it overwhelm you. While you may have to make some adjustments along the way, if you follow your step-by-step plan for achieving your goals, you will get there—and that lofty dream will be your new reality!

DAY 2
LONG LIVE
YOUR GROCERIES!

DAILY INSPIRATION

Day 2 is one of our favorites, because it takes all those grocery store items you just saved on and makes them last longer. Our storage secrets will have your food lasting way past their expiration dates.

While working through each day of the Money Diet, you may want to write your thoughts down in a journal. Get a notebook, or use your electronic calendar or note function on your phone and take a moment each day to write down your successes (and yes, times when you could have done better). On days when you're feeling down about your financial success, look back through your journal and remember the times you did well. Notice what patterns you see forming and make sure to congratulate yourself for the positive steps you take!

DAILY SAVINGS SUBJECT
Long Live Your Groceries!

If you feel like you're often throwing away spoiled food, you're going to love Day 2. We're going to show you how to make everything in your refrigerator last longer than you ever thought possible.

BIGGEST SAVER:
INVEST IN A CHEST FREEZER

If you have a garage, basement, or other suitable space in your home for a chest freezer, you can enjoy big savings. That's because when you find a great deal on a product, you can easily buy multiple items and save them for later.

End ordering out forever by making two of everything with items you find on sale and freezing for later: Not just casseroles, but burritos, spaghetti sauce, pizza dough, pancake batter, cooked French toast, meatballs, or anything else you can think of. Learn to butcher larger cuts of meat by looking up videos on YouTube or asking a foodie friend, and save at the store by buying meat in bulk. And did you know it's possible to freeze milk, cheese, and produce? When used in cooking or baking you'll never be able to tell the difference in taste.

The best thing about a chest freezer is that it uses a lot less energy than an upright freezer. This is because cold air is heavier than hot air, and tends to stay put when the door of a chest freezer opens up. Meanwhile, an upright freezer releases most of its cold air the minute the door is opened. Keep your eyes peeled at garage sales, secondhand stores like the Salvation Army, and on "free stuff" websites like Craigslist.org and Freecycle.org for free and inexpensive chest freezers.

WHO KNEW?   QUICK TIP

Milk sold at the local gas station or convenience store is cheaper than grocery store milk. They often mark down prices to get customers into the store. You could save $2 on every gallon.

Annual savings: $312.

GET THE AIR OUT

Air is your enemy when it comes to making sure your food lasts as long as possible. By simply removing the air from packages and containers, you can prolong the life of all sorts of items in your fridge. That means squeezing all of the air out of resealable bags before you seal them, making sure to tightly seal storage and other containers, and never leaving items uncovered in the fridge.

An easy way to make sure there isn't a lot of air in your containers is to make them smaller! Use the smallest-possible storage—make sure to save those margarine tubs, baby food jars, and anything else you can store food in. Then transfer food and even liquids like wine into smaller containers as you use them.

SIMPLE WAYS TO PROLONG
THE BIG STUFF

The biggest expenses in your fridge other than meat are dairy products and eggs. Here are some simple ways to prolong the life of these high-priced items.

- **Use small containers.** Mayonnaise, mustard, sour cream, yogurt, and other condiments will last longer if you move them into smaller containers as you use them up. The trick, of course, is making sure you successfully transfer every bit of mayo possible from the jar to the tiny container. We usually do our container downsizing right before we're about to use the condiment on something. That way, we can scrape out what we don't transfer to our sandwiches.

- **Save on milk.** It's better to store milk on an inside shelf toward the back of the refrigerator, not on the door. Why? The optimal refrigeration temperature of milk is actually just over 32°F; however, few refrigerators are ever set at (or hold) that low a temperature. Most home refrigerators remain around 40°F, and the temperature rises every time the door is opened.
- **Extend the life of milk.** Add a teaspoon of baking soda or a pinch of salt to each carton of milk—this alone will keep it fresh for a week or so past its expiration date! *POTENTIAL SAVINGS AMOUNT: $3 A GALLON.*
- **Save on cheese.** When storing cheese in the fridge, wrap it in a cloth dampened in white vinegar and put it in an airtight container near the bottom of the refrigerator, where temperature fluctuations are minimal. If you aren't going to use it for a while, add a few sugar cubes. If mold does form, it will form on the sugar cubes and not on the cheese. If mold does form on the

cheese, it can usually be safely cut off, as long as it's not a soft or shredded cheese. If it's a hard or semi-soft cheese like parmesan, cheddar, or Swiss, cut off the mold, leaving an additional 1 inch of cheese all around the mold. Make sure your knife doesn't touch the mold and contaminate the rest of the cheese. Throw away the moldy parts and don't tell any picky eaters what you just did!

- **Make sour cream last longer.** Add white vinegar right after you open your sour cream (1 teaspoon for a small container and 2 tablespoons for a large container). You won't notice the taste, and the sour cream won't go bad as quickly.
- **Save on eggs.** To keep your eggs lasting longer, don't store them on the door of your fridge, where temperature fluctuations could harm them. Turn the carton upside down before you store it, and your eggs will last even longer! Storing them upside down ensures the yolks don't touch the sides, which prolongs their life.

PRESERVING PRODUCE

Making sure that produce keeps for a long time is trickier than preserving dairy and other foods, because each different kind of fruit or vegetable has its own rules.

- **Keep fruits and veggies separate.** One rule to live by is to store fruit and vegetables in separate drawers in your fridge, with the fruit in one and the veggies in the other. Even when chilled, fruit gives off ethylene gas that shortens the shelf life of vegetables (and other fruit) by causing them to ripen more quickly.

WHO KNEW? **QUICK TIP**

Never wrap foods that contain natural acids—like tomatoes, lemons, or onions—in aluminum foil. The combination of the foil and the acid in the foods produces a chemical reaction, which affects the taste of the food.

- **Wrap all produce loosely.** Air circulation around fruits and vegetables reduces spoilage so wrap loosely. A sealed perforated plastic bag is ideal—but instead of buying them at the market, make your own by simply poking several holes in an ordinary sandwich or freezer bag. Line the crisper bins of your refrigerator with newspaper or a few paper towels to absorb excess moisture. (Mold spores love moisture, but the paper will keep it away.)

To make leafy herbs and vegetables like asparagus and broccoli last longer in the refrigerator, place the stem ends in a container of water, or wrap them in a wet paper towel and put in a plastic bag. Like flowers, the asparagus will continue "drinking" the water and stay fresh until they're ready to use.

- **Save on berries.** The moisture content of fresh berries and other fruit like grapes is high, so make sure to dry them thoroughly before you stick them in the fridge, or wait until you're ready to eat them before you wash them. Store berries, especially strawberries, loosely covered in the refrigerator. If you don't finish them, you can freeze them just when they start to turn overripe. Place them in a single layer on a cookie sheet and stick the sheet in the freezer. Once they're frozen, you can transfer them to a resealable plastic bag and save. It is cheaper to buy fruit in season and freeze it. If you go through a pint of berries a week, the potential for savings is tremendous. *SAVINGS AMOUNT: $3.99 FOR EACH CARTON OF BERRIES YOU FREEZE.*

- **Make lemons last.** Lemons will stay fresh for up to three months if you store them in a bowl of water in the fridge. Just change the water every week. If you have a bunch of lemons that are about to go bad, just freeze them! First cut in slices, then freeze on a baking sheet or in between pieces of wax paper. They're perfect for adding to glasses of water. Buying lemons on sale and keeping them for longer can save you a bit of cash. *SAVINGS AMOUNT: 50 CENTS A LEMON.*

- **Save on lettuce.** To make sure iceberg lettuce lasts as long as possible, you should remove the innermost core before you store it in the fridge. An easy (and admittedly fun) way to do this is to hit the lettuce against a hard surface and then twist the core out. This is preferable to cutting.

- **Save on mushrooms.** The best way to store mushrooms in the fridge? Leave them in their original container, uncovered except for a single layer of cheesecloth on top. To freeze mushrooms, wipe them off with a damp paper towel and slice them. Then sauté them in a small amount of butter or olive oil until they are almost done. Remove from the heat, allow them to cool, then place them in an airtight plastic bag in the freezer. They should keep for up to

10–12 months! ***SAVINGS AMOUNT: $1.99 FOR A CARTON OF MUSHROOMS.***

- **Save on onions.** The sugar content of yellow onions makes them spoil quickly if they are stored closely together—who knew? The solution is to store your onions in an old (clean) pair of pantyhose, making knots in the legs so the onions can't touch. It might look a little weird, but it works! You can also keep chopped onions in the freezer. Once you cook them you'll never be able to tell they've been frozen.

WHO KNEW? QUICK TIP

Place unripe tomatoes in a brown paper bag and leave them on your counter—they'll ripen in a day or two. If they're ripe already, store them in a cool place (around 55°F) and they'll keep for five days. In order to keep its membranes intact, you should never refrigerate a tomato!

Savings amount: $1–$1.50 for each tomato.

- **Save on peppers.** When using only part of a hot or sweet pepper, cut it from the bottom or the sides, leaving the seeds attached, and it will remain moist for longer. You can put the rest in a resealable plastic bag and use it up to 3–4 days later. *SAVINGS AMOUNT: $0.99 FOR EACH PEPPER.*

- **Save on potatoes.** Here's a fun trick: If you store fresh ginger with potatoes it will help keep them fresh longer!

DAY 2
FINANCIAL FITNESS PLAN
Organizing Your Financial Records

Today's Financial Fitness Plan is easier than it sounds: Just grab all those bills that you've been avoiding and put them in a pile. Don't worry about what they say for now—today is all about getting them in shape so you can start to get a sense of your financial picture. While you're at it, get your unopened mail, that stack of paper on your desk, and any other papers you've been "meaning to get to." We're about to give you a cheat sheet that will tell you what to do with it all!

You may want to use some file folders, hanging files, or an accordion file to organize your records. Or just use paperclips and Post-It Notes. No matter what you decide, begin by opening all the envelopes and sorting everything into piles. Then turn the piles into files and you can throw everything else away! Here is what you need to keep:

- **Bills.** Later on, we'll be figuring out how much you usually spend on each bill. You can do that by either accessing your account history online, or saving two or three statements from each company now. If you've paid the bill, throw it away unless you need to save it for tax purposes (like if you work from home).

- **Bank and credit card statements.** Save your current statement until you get next month's statement, and then shred it and throw it away. Banks can provide you with past statements and check images if necessary. For investment accounts, also save documents that contain your investment options and your summary plan description, correspondence with any financial planners, and annual summaries.
- **Employment documents.** Save all contracts and employee agreements that you have signed. It's also a good idea to keep all of your past employee evaluations as well as employee rules or handbooks. If you are planning on moving or applying for a loan sometime soon, keep 6 months' worth of pay stubs.
- **Education records.** Keep diplomas, transcripts, and enrollment records.
- **Auto documents.** Make a folder for your cars' titles and any maintenance records. Keep a copy of your insurance agreement and your most recent statement.

- **Home documents.** Save warranties and receipts for all major purchases, as well as invoices and records regarding home improvements and repairs that you've made.
- **Health records.** Save medical records and vaccination records for all members of your family, including your pets.
- **Tax documents.** Keep receipts for anything you plan on writing off in the current year, along with W2 forms and 1099s. You should save past tax returns for at least three years.

DAY 3
CLEAN UP YOUR SPENDING

DAILY INSPIRATION

The average American family of four spends between $800 and $900 a year on cleaning products and related supplies, according to the U.S. Bureau of Labor Statistics. That's a lot of money! But with the clever and creative cleaning solutions you learn today, you can dramatically reduce—and nearly eliminate—this expenditure! As an added bonus, many of our tips are safer for your family and have a less toxic effect on the environment than their expensive commercial counterparts. It's a win-win situation!

Today it's time to acknowledge the fears and doubts that may be holding you back. It's okay to admit that you're a little scared! Remind yourself that you've already taken the bravest step: making the commitment to financial fitness. Now take 20 minutes and write down your money anxieties. Don't hold back; you don't have to share this list with anyone else. You may not have openly acknowledged your concerns before, but it's important that you do, so that you can start to address them. Once you've got your list, step back for a moment. Look carefully at each concern and list several practical ways you can start addressing it. By seeking solutions, you can clear a pathway to financial fitness.

DAILY SAVINGS SUBJECT
Clean Up Your Spending

CUT COSTS IN THE KITCHEN

Check out the cleaning product aisle in your grocery store and you'll see how many products there are to spend money on. From wasteful paper products to expensive specialty cleansers, it's easy to waste money trying to keep your home clean. Try these thrifty, natural tips to save a bundle:

- **Stop using paper towels.** When your toddler spills your iced tea and you don't want to waste a bunch of paper towels mopping it up, use old clothes that you've cut into rags. They're free and you can wash them, so they're less harmful to the environment. If you use one to two rolls of paper towels a week, at an average cost of $1.50–2.00 per roll, you could save $100 or more every year. *ANNUAL SAVINGS: $78–208.*

- **Save on Swiffer.** Just because you have a wet/dry mop like Swiffer doesn't mean you have to spend a cent on those pricey replacement cloths! Instead, use a sock from your "missing mates" pile and stretch it around the head of the mop. It will work just as well, and you can throw it in the washing machine when you're done! ***ANNUAL SAVINGS: $85.***

- **Double the life of your sponges.** Don't toss out a smelly sponge! To quickly kill the dangerous bacteria that make a home in your kitchen sponge, wring it out, then microwave it on high for 30–60 seconds. (Don't nuke a dry sponge, or it might ignite.) If you use a new sponge every two weeks, you could cut your annual costs in half or more. We also like to cut a new sponge in half and make it last even longer! Or ditch the sponges entirely and switch to dishcloths you can just toss in the wash and reuse. ***ANNUAL SAVINGS: $13–$26.***

- **Clean the oven without harsh chemicals.** A simple way to clean your oven is to place an oven-safe pot or bowl filled with water inside. Heat on 450°F for 20 minutes, and steam will loosen the dirt and grease. Once your oven is cool, wipe off the condensation and the grease will come with it. When you're done, make a paste of water and baking soda and smear it on any enamel. The paste will dry into a protective layer that will absorb grease as you cook. If you clean your oven twice a year, you avoid buying two bottles of oven cleaner. **SAVINGS AMOUNT: $14.**

WHO KNEW? QUICK TIP

A good all-purpose cleaner is easy to make with stuff you already have. Start with 1/4 gallon water and mix in 1/2 cup rubbing alcohol, a squirt of dishwashing liquid, and 3/4 teaspoon ammonia (nonsudsy). Fill a spray bottle and you're ready to clean.

Annual savings: $36.

- **Get the gunk off your stove.** Brew a pot of tea that is four times normal strength, then wipe it on your stove. The tannins in the tea will make it hard for grease and food to stick, making cleaning quick and easy. **ANNUAL SAVINGS: $36.**
- **Make mops like new.** You can revive porous cleaning materials, like the head of your mop, with a little salt. Fill a bucket with a mixture of 1/4 cup salt and 1 quart warm water. Then soak your mops and sponges for 8–10 hours and the grunge will be gone. **SAVINGS AMOUNT: $4 PER MOP HEAD.**

- **Perk up your floor.** If you have black scuff marks on your linoleum or vinyl flooring, you can remove them with a bit of white (non-gel) toothpaste. Simply rub the toothpaste over the scuff vigorously until it disappears. You can also try this with a pink pencil eraser!

WHO KNEW?　　　　**QUICK TIP**

Is there anything more satisfying than nice, clean grout? A simple paste of three parts baking soda and one part water is all you need. Make a new batch each time you plan to attack the spaces between your tiles and around your tub.

Savings amount: $7.49 on grout cleaner.

FIND BIG SAVINGS IN THE BATHROOM

Between mold, mildew, and unpleasant odors, the bathroom can be one of the grimiest areas of the house. Fortunately, we've found some natural and effective ways to tackle this tough job without robbing your pocketbook.

- **Make your own daily shower spray.** Stay on top of mold and mildew by keeping this daily shower spray within easy reach of all family members. Mix one part vinegar with 10 parts water in an empty spray bottle and you're ready to go.

Bonus: You don't have to worry about a toxic cleaner hitting the baby's bath toys. ***SAVINGS AMOUNT: $4 PER BOTTLE.***

- **Get rid of grout stains.** After the last person of the day has showered, apply shaving cream to the grout and leave it on until the first shower the next day! Repeat for a day or two and your grout stains will be gone. Best of all, shaving cream doesn't contain bleach so it's less harsh on your grout! ***SAVINGS AMOUNT: $3.***

- **Extend the life of your shower curtain.** If you have a pair of pinking shears (scissors with a zigzagging edge used in sewing), put them to good use in the bathroom. Use them to cut the bottom of your shower curtain liner: The uneven hem allows water to more easily slide off, making bottom-of-the-curtain mildew a thing of the past. ***SAVINGS AMOUNT: $10-$20 PER SHOWER CURTAIN.***

- **Don't buy toilet bowl cleaner.** For a cheap and easy way to clean your toilet, use mouthwash. Just pour a capful into the bowl, leave for 10-15 minutes, and wipe clean with your toilet brush. ***SAVINGS AMOUNT: $3-$4.***

WHO KNEW?   **QUICK TIP**

Save those little lime and lemon juice bottles and use them to clean computer keyboards, electronics, and other items with tiny crevices. Wash the containers well and let them dry completely before using them as tools for puffing away dust and dirt. You'll never have to buy compressed air containers. ***Savings amount: $4-$6.***

TACKLE THE REST OF THE HOUSE

Did you know that you can polish brass with Worcestershire sauce? That lemon dissolves mineral deposits in faucets, and white bread removes all kinds of stains (even ink!) from wallpaper? You can also rub away a marker stain on carpet with rubbing alcohol, and remove water marks from wood with Vaseline. From dusting to cleaning windows, here are more great tips for a sparkling clean home without spending a lot of dough.

- **Make your own lemon oil.** Save money on wood cleaners by making your own at home. It's simple: Just combine the juice from one lemon with 2 cups vegetable or olive oil. Use it just like you would use a store-bought cleaner! You may need to shake before using each time. *SAVINGS AMOUNT: $3-$4 PER BOTTLE.*
- **Clean glass with cornstarch.** To clean dirty windows—or even your car's windshield—mix a tablespoon of cornstarch with about 1/2 gallon of warm water, apply to the windows, and dry with a soft cloth. It's amazing how quickly the dirt is removed—and no streaking, either!
- **It's a breeze to eliminate odors.** Here's an easy spray that will completely neutralize household odors for mere pennies. Fill a two-cup spray bottle with water and add 2 tablespoons baking soda. Shake before spritzing. You can also add your favorite essential oil for a fresh scent! *SAVINGS AMOUNT: $3-$4 PER BOTTLE.*
- **Dust with dryer sheets.** Don't throw away used dryer sheets! You can reuse them to dust your home. They're also great for cleaning glass in the shower. *SAVINGS AMOUNT: $7-$15.*

WHO KNEW? **QUICK TIP**

Stop buying expensive plug-in air freshener refills. You can buy essential oils online and make a much cheaper alternative. Just remove the wick from the bulb, add water and a few drops of essential oil. Replace the wick, plug in, and enjoy!

Annual savings: $20–$30.

DAY 3
FINANCIAL FITNESS PLAN
Talking to Your Spouse About Money

Disagreements over money are one of the main causes of marital discord—and divorce—in this country. For today's Financial Fitness plan, we discuss how to navigate these thorny issues, so that you and your spouse or partner can start working *with* each other, not *against* each other. In order to improve your financial situation, you both need to be on board with a plan for debt reduction. After all, it doesn't do much good to cut $50 out of your monthly cleaning budget if you or your partner go out and spend that savings on a few DVDs or a new pair of shoes. Plus, if you work together, you can help keep each other on track and provide encouragement! Here are some tips for getting the conversation started:

- **Pick a good time.** Don't discuss money after a bad day at the office, when you're about to go to bed, or during another argument. Choose a time when you're both relaxed and in a good mood! You'll increase your chances of success.

- **Keep it positive.** You may feel that your spouse or partner deserves most of the blame for your financial situation, but if you start lashing out, you're likely to turn the other person against you and start a fight. Begin by taking responsibility for your own financial missteps. The other person may soon admit his or her own failings as well!

- **Get your spouse on board.** You may have come up with your own particular plan for getting out of debt, but if you impose it on your partner without getting feedback first, you're likely to meet with strong resistance. Instead use words like, "I've come up with some ideas for how we can start cutting our expenses and paying down our debt. I'd love to discuss them with you and see what you think." Then listen to the response without interrupting. Try to stay as non-confrontational as possible.

- **Take a break.** If things start to get heated, take a break and set a time to come back and discuss the issue again later! Don't leave it open ended. If you still can't come to an agreement, you might want to enlist a third party like a financial planner or a counselor to help. Sometimes there are underlying issues that are causing these spending issues that only a counselor can help unravel.

DAY 4
BEAUTIFY ON A BUDGET

DAILY INSPIRATION

Do you spend tons of money on the latest beauty products? Stop! Today we'll help you learn how to lengthen the life of your cosmetics, and save money on your beauty essentials.

Today is the day to be open to the wisdom of others. It could be anyone whose opinion you trust: a friend, a family member, or a coworker. Maybe it's your neighbor with the beautiful folio of alphabetized coupons or the guy who reads *Consumer Reports* like it's a thriller novel. Be open to the good habits and opinions that surround you. Don't be embarrassed to ask someone else's opinion when you need it, and don't be afraid to reciprocate and share your own wisdom—like the tips you learn in this chapter—with those around you.

WHO KNEW?   QUICK TIP

Replace expensive travel-size items with freebies like the beauty supply samples offered at KillerFreebies.com.

Savings amount: $10 per trip.

DAILY SAVINGS SUBJECT
Beautify on a Budget

Most women love beauty products, but they also know how expensive they can be. Fortunately, there are many affordable brands out there, as well as many ways to extend the life of the products you have or buy. You can also make some products at home with items you probably already have in your pantry. Today we'll help you stop draining your wallet on new mascara every month and start saving!

BIG SAVER: GET EVERY LAST DROP

Do you hate not being able to get to the last bit of moisturizer in the bottle? Or maybe your mascara dries up too quickly. Use these tips and tricks to get the most out of your cosmetics.

- **Save on mascara.** Mascara starting to dry out? Just add several drops of saline eye drops and shake. The eye drops will keep the mascara lasting much longer than you ever thought possible! *SAVINGS AMOUNT: $10.*

WHO KNEW?   QUICK TIP

Did you know that on average, antiperspirants and deodorants made for men are $3 cheaper than their female counterparts— even when they have the same ingredients? If you're a woman who uses unscented deodorant, opt for the guys' stuff instead to save! You may also find a lightly scented variety you like.

Savings amount: $3.

- **Double your foundation.** Some of the most expensive makeup is foundation and powder. Make them last longer by buying a shade darker than your natural one, then mixing it with moisturizer (for foundation), or baby powder (for powder) until it matches your normal color. You'll have more than twice as much, and you'll never be able to tell the difference! *SAVINGS AMOUNT: $30.*

- **De-clump your mascara.** When your mascara starts to clump, you don't have to toss it out! Smooth it out again by setting the tube in a teacup of near-boiling water for five minutes. *SAVINGS AMOUNT: $10.*

- **Re-press powder.** Oh no! You just dropped your compact, and now your powder is in a million tiny pieces. To get any kind of powder makeup (such as foundation, eye shadow, or blush) back together again, add a few drops of rubbing alcohol to the fine dust, then push it back together with the back of a spoon. Your powder will become pressed again!

- **Protect makeup from the sun.** Many forms of makeup are sensitive to the sun due to their preservatives. Keep your makeup away from the window so it lasts as long as possible.
- **Extend your razors' life.** The next time you open something that has one of those little silica gel packets in it, save them for your bathroom. Store your razor near these little wonders (like in the bottom of a cup) and they'll soak up any remaining moisture that has been left on the blades. It's minuscule rust that dulls the blades, so they'll last months longer. ***ANNUAL SAVINGS: $8.***

WHO KNEW?   QUICK TIP

Baby shampoo is an inexpensive way to remove mascara, eyeliner, and eyeshadow. It contains many of the same ingredients as eye make-up remover and works just as well, but costs a lot less. Pour a small amount on a tissue or cotton ball, rub over closed eyes, and rinse with water.

Savings amount: $22.

MAKE IT YOURSELF!

Cosmetics can be pretty pricey, so why not save some money by making your own products at home? It's easy to use pantry products for items like self-tanner and body scrub. Just read on for our favorites!

- **Save on hair dye.** If you have dark hair, you can conceal grays without having to pay for hair dye. Just rinse your hair with strong coffee (let it cool first!). Let the coffee sit in your hair for 3 minutes, then rinse out. Repeat one or two times as necessary. The coffee will not only provide a subtle tint, it will get rid of any product build-up on your locks! If you're going to the salon to get the job done, you could save hundreds per year! *ANNUAL SAVINGS: UP TO $300.*

- **Make your own blotter.** Going green (and saving money!) means replacing disposable household products with reusable ones. If you still use a paper towel or toilet paper to blot your make-up brushes, replace them with a pale-colored bathroom or kitchen tile. The tile is perfect for seeing color before you apply it, and it's easy to clean. When you're ready to put it away, just run warm water over it and let air-dry!

- **Make your own bath salts.** Here's an easy way to have a relaxing soak in a bath without having to buy bath salts. Just place one or two green tea bags under the faucet as you fill up your bath. The antioxidants in the tea will leave your skin feeling fresh. ***ANNUAL SAVINGS: $30.***

- **Tan with tea!** For an all-natural self-tanner, use black tea. Brew two cups of tea with 10 teabags and let cool. Then pour into a spray bottle and spray onto clean, dry skin and let dry. Repeat as often as you'd like! ***SAVINGS AMOUNT: $10–$20 A BOTTLE.***

- **Use dish liquid as hand soap.** These days, most dishwashing liquids have moisturizers in them to keep your hands smooth even after doing the dishes. They work so well, you can use dishwashing liquid as a stand-in for those expensive pump hand soaps! Just fill an old soap dispenser with 2 tablespoons dishwashing liquid and top off with water. Shake to combine and you'll have hand soap at a fraction of the cost. ***SAVINGS AMOUNT: $2 PER DISPENSER.***

- **Stop buying special moisturizers.** Whether it's night cream, day cream, anti-aging lotion, or anti-wrinkle solution, all moisturizers have most of the same ingredients. Pick an affordable brand moisturizer with an SPF of at least 15. Trader Joe's brand is a personal favorite! Your wallet will know the difference, but your face never will.

- **Switch to baby wipes.** You should never leave make-up on overnight, as it can dry out your skin (and leave marks on your pillow!). One of the quickest ways to remove cosmetics is with a pre-moistened wipe, but skip the expensive make-up removal wipes and keep of stash of baby wipes near the sink instead. The next time you come home after a late night, rub one over your face before you hit the sack. ***ANNUAL SAVINGS: $60.***
- **Use milk as a face treatment.** Looking for a fabulous age-defying skin treatment? Check your fridge: Milk is nutritious for your insides *and* your outsides. Lactic acid works as an exfoliant, and milk's amino acids and proteins have a calming effect on red skin. Just dab onto skin with a clean cloth. Stick to fat-free milk for the best results.

WHO KNEW?   QUICK TIP

Large-granule sugar is an excellent exfoliant that can be mixed with any regular cleanser. Try brown sugar, if you have it; it's not as processed as white sugar. Consider stirring in a bit of olive oil, which has wonderful moisturizing and anti-inflammatory properties. Enjoy your homemade body scrub and saved money!

Savings amount: at least $6 a container.

- **Use avocado as a leave-in conditioner.** Dry, brittle, limp hair will be a thing of the past after using this simple leave-in hair mask recipe featuring nourishing avocados. This is especially helpful for color-treated hair that's looking fried. In a medium bowl, beat one egg and then add 1/2 cup of olive oil and 1/3 cup of yogurt. Mash one avocado in a separate bowl and then add to other mixture and stir to combine; it's okay if the mixture is chunky. Apply to dry hair and massage into roots. Leave on for 25 minutes and then rinse with lukewarm water. Wash hair with shampoo and conditioner as usual. *ANNUAL SAVINGS: AT LEAST $30.*

- **Make your own bubble bath.** You don't need expensive bath gels to get a luxurious bubble bath. To make your own bubble bath, simply place soap slivers in a mesh drawstring bag. (To get soap slivers, use a vegetable peeler on a sturdy bar of soap, or just keep left over soap ends and reuse them this way.) Attach the bag to the tap while the water is running. For even more fragrance, put a couple of drops of your favorite essential oil in the bag, or herbs like rosemary and thyme. *ANNUAL SAVINGS: AT LEAST $25.*

- **Save on face cream.** Want to save a ton of money on face cream? Just take the peel of an avocado and lightly wipe the inside of it across your face. Your face will love all the natural oils! You can rinse your face after 15 minutes or leave on overnight for extremely dry skin. *ANNUAL SAVINGS: AT LEAST $50.*

MAXIMIZING YOUR BEAUTY BUDGET

Of course, you will need to buy new makeup and cosmetics from time to time. But you want to make sure those products are practical and cost effective.

- **Get the best price on makeup.** When shopping for makeup and other cosmetics, never ever shop at upscale department stores! Because of sales commissions and the cost to rent the space at the store, they're never a bargain. Instead, check out your local grocery store or discount store such as Walmart or Target—they almost always have the exact same brands for much less. If you can't find them there, try to find a cosmetics discount outlet such as Ulta, or search for "discount cosmetics" online. If you still can't find your brand, consider switching to another brand you *can* find. Choose one a good friend uses, and ask her if she'd be willing to buy it from you if you don't like it. It shouldn't be too hard to find one you like just as much that costs much less. *SAVINGS AMOUNT: $3–$20 PER PRODUCT.*

- **Trade in your unwanted makeup.** Did you know that if you're unhappy with your purchase, most chain drugstores will let you return even opened makeup? If your store won't accept the return, you can still get some money back by putting it up for trade on MakeupAlley.com's Swap Page!

- **Save at Sephora.** Another great place to shop is Sephora—if you buy their brand. Sephora offers a wide variety of name-brand beauty products, but their real deals are offered on their own line of cosmetics. Get a free birthday gift simply for registering for their "Beauty Insider" program. The gift varies from year to year, but you'll be sure to get a high-quality bath product, cosmetic, or skin-care item. You can also get other free products for spending money in their stores or online. Just go to Sephora.com/beautyinsider for more info. Go to Sephora.com and click on "Sign up for Sephora" to register. *SAVINGS AMOUNT: $1–$5 PER ITEM.*

- **Try makeup for free!** A great way to get free make-up as well as bonus gifts like a $50 Amazon.com gift card is by joining PinkPanel, a company that connects beauty companies with product testers. To sign up, visit Facebook.com/thePinkPanel and click on "Join PinkPanel." Then like their Facebook page to get updates about beauty product testing opportunities!

- **Swap used containers for new cosmetics!** Want more free stuff? Many cosmetics retailers now offer free products in return for bringing in empty make-up containers. M.A.C, for instance, will give you a free lipstick for returning six M.A.C. containers, while Lush gives you a free face mask for every five empty Lush containers you return. Kiehl's has a special card just for recycling Kiehl's containers, and has various rewards depending on the number of empty containers you return. Our favorite make-up recycling program comes from Origins. Bring a container from *any* make-up (regardless of brand) and get a free Origins skin-care sample! *SAVINGS AMOUNT: $7–$15.*
- **Collect free samples.** Get more free stuff and keep your skin soft and smooth with free samples and coupons at Oil of Olay (Olay.com/olay-coupons) and Dove (Dove.us/#/Offers/freesamples). You can also sign up for email newsletters that will keep you apprised of deals and special offers.

DAY 4
FINANCIAL FITNESS PLAN
Avoid Going Further into Debt

Gather your credit card bills from the last few months and ask yourself some tough questions. Examine your purchases—were they necessary? Are you consistently paying your monthly balance or just sending in the minimum payment? What is your limit—are you dangerously close to it? If so you risk getting charged extra fees and higher interest rates. Paying off your credit card in full each month is the best way to ward off out-of-control debt. Most of us know this, but few of us take the necessary steps to conquer their credit card issues. Here are some of those steps:

- **Transfer your balance to lower-interest cards.** Look for 0 percent interest credit card promotions in the mail. (But be sure to read the fine print in case there are hidden fees. Even a change from 25 percent interest to 20 percent interest can get you significant savings.)

- **Make biweekly payments.** If you are being charged interest on a daily basis, splitting your monthly payments into two equal biweekly payments will save you from a portion of those interest charges. Check with your credit card company to see if this is an option.
- **Avoid late fees whenever possible.** If you have trouble remembering the due date time, add a reminder to your calendar a few days before your due date. Go ahead and do it right now so you are never late again!
- **Golden rule: Pay more than the minimum if your finances allow.** Don't think you will make much progress on paying off the credit card if you stick to the monthly minimum. You'll feel like you're running in place. Make a slightly bigger payment on your highest-interest credit card this month, and rest easy knowing you'll be clear of your debt that much sooner.
- **Ask for a lower rate.** As long as you have a good credit history, it's OK to call and simply ask if your credit card company will lower your rate. In this economy, you may not get what you want. But it can't hurt to ask!

Once you've completely paid off your cards, you can start applying that money to your emergency fund and toward big-ticket items that you need to save up for—don't return to your previous routine of spending money you don't have!

It's important to remain disciplined with your budget, even after your debt has been paid off. Once that happens, you can begin to accumulate wealth, giving you true financial freedom.

DAY 5

MAXIMIZE YOUR CLOTHING BUDGET

DAILY INSPIRATION

Today we will focus on extending the life of your clothes and finding great deals. If you like to buy a new wardrobe at the start of each new season then you'll appreciate our tips for the storage, upkeep, repair, and purchasing of both adults' and children's clothing and shoes.

Before we get down to business, take a moment to consider whether you are honest with yourself about your spending habits. Without honesty, you are not truly committed to your Money Diet. If you tell yourself that you spend $100 a month on groceries, but your receipts tell a different (scarier) story, then you are setting yourself up for failure. Consider starting a spending journal if you haven't already. Writing down everything you purchase will help you ensure that your imagined spending is in line with your true spending. If you haven't actually started one yet, now is the time to commit to the habit. It will show you whether your imagined spending is in line with your true spending.

WHO KNEW?   QUICK TIP

Are the cuffs of your favorite sweater starting to get stretched out? Make them like new again by using a hot air dryer! Just wet the cuffs with water, set the hairdryer on its highest setting, and then blow-dry until the cuffs are no longer wet. The heat will shrink the cuffs slightly, bringing them back down to the right size.

Savings amount: $100 for a new cashmere sweater.

DAILY SAVINGS SUBJECT
Maximize Your Clothing Budget

Proper care and storage of your wardrobe is very important. Below, we share our favorite tips for cleaning and storage, plus lots of ways to save on laundry expenses. And when you do need to buy something new, we'll help make sure you get the best value!

BIG SAVER: PROPER CARE AND CLEANING

Every time you wear and launder an item there is potential for damage. These tips will help extend the life of the clothes you already have, make buying new ones less of a necessity, and save you tons of money. Keep an open mind about repairing old things rather than buying new ones, because this flexible attitude will do wonders for your finances in all areas.

- **Wear and re-wear your clothes.** For example, you can wear jeans and dark pants several times before washing. When you wash darks, use cold water and a short cycle, and air-dry if possible.

Sweaters and knits don't need to be washed after each wear. Before you throw in a load, turn knitted clothes and T-shirts with designs on them inside out. Since the average cost of doing a load of laundry is $1.50, this could save you $3 a week! **ANNUAL SAVINGS: $156.**

- **Stop the dryer early.** Take your cotton and denim clothing, and anything containing spandex, which can lose its elasticity when exposed to too much heat, out of the dryer 10–20 minutes before the cycle ends and let it air dry the rest of the way. Excess dryer heat can break down the fibers in your clothes prematurely. If this one simple tip means you can avoid buying three pairs of jeans every year, you can save hundreds! *SAVINGS AMOUNT: $150 FOR THREE PAIRS OF JEANS.*

- **Dry clean at home!** Don't bother taking wool, cashmere, and silk to the dry cleaners, which can be expensive and damaging over time. Instead, wash it at home. Wash wool with mild dishwashing liquid in cold water on the gentle cycle of your washing machine. If it's a blanket, air fluff to dry. If it's a garment, handle with great care, since wool fibers are very weak when wet. To get rid of excess water, don't pull, stretch, or wring out the garment. Instead, roll it in a towel, squeeze the excess water out, and then dry flat. For cashmere, use lukewarm water and a mild soap to wash by hand. Dry the same way you would dry wool. Silk should be hand-washed using cool water with mild liquid soap. Always air dry silk—never place it in the dryer, even on cool—and if you need to, iron it from the "wrong" side of the fabric. *MONTHLY SAVINGS: $75.*

- **Keep jeans from shrinking.** Jeans are usually tight enough as it is! To minimize shrinking, wash them in cold water, dry them on medium heat for only 10 minutes, and then air dry them the rest of the way. *SAVINGS AMOUNT: $50 PER PAIR OF JEANS.*

WHO KNEW? QUICK TIP

Do you have a jacket, backpack, or tent that used to be water resistant, but has lost its effectiveness over time? Set your hair dryer to its highest setting and blow air evenly over it. The warmth will reactivate the coating on the cloth that makes it repel water.

Savings amount: $100 per jacket.

- **Add coffee to keep blacks black.** If your black cotton items are starting to look more like they're dark blue, wash a load of only black items. But first, brew a strong pot of black coffee, and add it to the rinse cycle.
- **Put cashmere in the freezer.** If your favorite cashmere or angora sweater is looking a little worn, put it in a plastic bag and place it in the freezer for half an hour. The cold causes the fibers to expand, making your sweater look new again, saving you from buying a pricy new one. *SAVINGS AMOUNT: $100 PER SWEATER.*
- **Preserve Your Bras.** Rotate through your bras rather than wearing one for a few days in a row. You'll give the elastic time to contract and the bras will last longer. *SAVINGS AMOUNT: $30 PER BRA.*
- **Protect your leather shoes!** To extend the life of shoes that have leather soles, take them to a cobbler and ask him to put on rubber protectors, which will shield against water absorption and general wear and tear. They cost about $20 but will make your shoes last two or three years longer. *ANNUAL SAVINGS: $150.*

ERADICATING STAINS

Making stains vanish will save you tons of money in new clothes. Our favorite stain solutions may be surprising, but don't worry—they work!

- **Apply astringent to ring around the collar!** If your dress shirts are getting stained around the collar, wipe the back of your neck with an alcohol-based astringent before you get dressed in the morning. The alcohol will prevent your sweat from leaving a stain. *SAVINGS AMOUNT: $120 FOR THREE SHIRTS.*

- **Treat ties tenderly.** Never try to remove a stain from a tie with water or you may create a large watermark that's hard to remove. Blot away excess stains with a napkin or soft, white cloth. Take it to the dry cleaner as soon as possible: stains set after 24 to 48 hours. Don't attempt to rub the stain out or you could rub color from the fabric, especially if it's silk. *SAVINGS AMOUNT: $30 PER TIE.*

- **Blot your stains.** If you get a stain on something dark, make sure to blot it instead of rubbing, which will cause it to lighten and show more.

- **Soak and bag stains for easy removal.** Don't let a stain "set" even if you are running out the door. Instead, spray with stain remover or soak in water and store in a resealable plastic bag until you have time to deal with it. Once a stain dries, it's much harder to remove.

- **Use the toothbrush trick.** Have a mystery stain you can't get out? Try using the old toothbrush trick. First, apply some dishwashing liquid, or even just some laundry detergent, to the stain. Then rub it in with an old toothbrush for about 30 seconds. The toothbrush will help penetrate the fibers of your clothes, even getting out worn-in stains.

WHO KNEW? **QUICK TIP**

Here's a great tip to prevent those pesky yellow stains on the armpits of your white shirts. Coat the would-be stained area on the inside of the shirt with a spray adhesive (available at your local craft store). The adhesive will seal the fibers, so that sweat and your deodorant can't get inside them—or stain the cloth. You can also try sprinkling on a little baby powder before you iron the spot.

Savings amount: $40 per dress shirt.

MAXIMIZING YOUR LAUNDRY BUDGET

Buying all that detergent and fabric softener can get expensive! Not to mention just running the washer and dryer themselves. Here are a few ways to use what you have at home and minimize machine run time to save money and energy.

- **Use white vinegar as a fabric softener.** Instead of fabric softener, simply use white vinegar. Use the same proportions as you would for a liquid fabric softener—you'll never notice the difference. You can also use a clean kitchen sponge dampened with liquid fabric softener instead of one of those balls that releases fabric softener. Just put it in the washing machine once it's filled with water at the beginning of the load. It will slowly release the softener, just like the plastic balls do! *SAVINGS AMOUNT: $25.*

- **Make detergent for delicates.** There's no need to spend money on detergents just for delicates. Instead, use this homemade solution: 1 cup baking soda mixed with 1 cup warm water. The baking soda will clean your clothes without harming their delicate fibers. *SAVINGS AMOUNT: $15.*

- **Don't overstuff your washer!** It might seem more cost-effective to stuff your washing machine to the brim, but it's actually less efficient—the clothes rub against each other more, and the water doesn't have as much room to flush away dirt and oils. For the best wash, only fill your washing machine three-fourths full. This gives your clothes enough room to get fully clean.

- **Empty your pockets.** Make sure all the pockets of your pants and shirts are empty before washing and drying them. Items like pieces of paper, dollar bills, and other similar materials create more lint in your dryer filter, making dry times even longer.

WHO KNEW? **QUICK TIP**

Using cold water to wash your laundry loads is a simple way to save a lot of money. Unless you're dealing with some seriously soiled clothing, most loads will get completely clean using cold water. Aside from upping your energy costs, using warm or hot water also wears down your clothes faster, so the savings are even greater!

Annual Savings: $214.

- **Use the sun as your dryer.** Air-drying your clothes is the best way to save a lot of money on energy costs. If you have the space, either inside or outside, air-dry as many clothes as possible. *ANNUAL SAVINGS: $205.*
- **Put a dry towel in with wet clothes.** If you must use a dryer, add a big, dry towel to the machine

when drying jeans and other bulky items. It will cut the drying time significantly.

SAFE STORAGE

Now that you've taken such good care of your clothes, it's time to make sure they stay in good shape while in storage. You will save tons of money when you avoid buying all new sweaters next winter.

- **Avoid airtight storage.** When storing your winter clothes for the season, don't place them in an airtight container, which will trap moisture inside and can lead to mildew spores forming. Instead, use an old duffel bag or suitcase. If you don't have one available, wrap your clothes in a large sheet and knot it at the top. Wrap sweaters in newspaper and tape the sides. The newspaper will keep away both moths and moisture.
- **Don't store leather in plastic.** When storing leather and suede garments, don't cover them in plastic. These materials need a little breathing space, or they'll quickly dry out.
- **Throw away dry-cleaner bags!** Never store clothing that's come from the dry cleaners in the plastic sheath they return it in. It will keep the chemicals used at the cleaners enclosed around your garment, which can damage the fabric of your clothing.

SHOPPING TO YOUR POTENTIAL

Of course, you will need to buy new clothes from time
to time. But you want to make sure you're getting the
best prices. Here are some tips:

- **Join the club.** Did you know that many department stores (like Saks Fifth Avenue, Nordstrom,
  and Lord & Taylor) offer unadvertised, online-
  only sales to their e-mail subscribers? Sign up
  and you'll receive friends-and-family promotions, too (usually 25 percent off). ***ANNUAL
  SAVINGS: $750.***

- **Put that AAA card to work!** You can also save
  up to 15 percent with your AAA card at retailers like Target.com, New York & Company, and
  more. Visit aaa.com for more details. ***ANNUAL
  SAVINGS: $300.***

- **Compare prices.** Use cell phone applications like Google Shopper and websites like Nextag.com to get the savviest price before you make each purchase.
- **Get a credit card.** Credit cards from companies like Amazon will reward your everyday purchases with spending points and give extra rewards when you purchase items at their store. You can use your earned points to get next month's clothing for free!

WHO KNEW?   QUICK TIP

For the best deals on clothes, always shop in the off-season. Buy spring and summer clothing in July and August, and fall and winter clothing in January and February. (You can often find the best sales right after the holiday season.) Last year, a friend bought a $150 bathing suit for $40.

Potential savings amount: $110 or more.

- **Bargain and thrift stores are your friends.** How many times have you purchased an $80 sweater, only to find a nearly identical one later for much less? When you begin to look for clothes for the new season, always start at the least expensive store first. Since most clothing stores carry similar items each season, you'll make sure to get each piece for the best price. Try to limit your purchases to practical items, but if you have to have the latest, trendiest garment, get it at a cheaper store like Forever 21 or H&M. Always take gently used items to consignment shops or thrift stores to get some money back, or trade them for new (used) clothes. One person's trash is another's treasure!

- **Sale schedule.** If you're shopping in your favorite store and notice that there are tons of markdowns, go home and mark the day on your calendar. Most stores receive shipments of new goods every 9–12 weeks and discount current merchandise to make room for the new stuff. Return to the store during that time frame to find more deals.

DAY 5
FINANCIAL FITNESS PLAN
Examining Your Finances

On Day 3, you got your financial records organized. Now it's time to see what they say—even though it might be scary! As you go through your records, remember to focus on improvement, not on feeling bad about the debt you might be in. Remember, we're going to help you get out of it!

1. Before you dive into the nitty gritty, write down your financial goals for the future. They could be early retirement, paying off your mortgage, or taking that trip to Paris. Always keep these goals at the forefront of your mind so you remember what you're working toward. It may even be help-ful to write goals on sticky notes and stick them around your house—or in your wallet—to keep your eyes on the prize and off that expensive but unnecessary new stereo.

2. Next, check your emergency fund. What would happen if one of the earners in your household

was unable to work? Most experts recommend having six months of expenses saved up for emergencies. Determine what you spend on food and shelter each month and then multiply by six. This amount may seem daunting, so start by using direct deposit to funnel $25 from your salary each pay period into a separate account. If you feel comfortable with that, up the amount to $50, $100, or as much as you feel is possible.

3. If the interest rates for your mortgage and credit cards are variable, keep track of them closely, as well as the rates on the market. Mortgage rates happen to be at the lowest in years so examine your situation and determine whether it makes sense to refinance. For credit cards, move all your debt to the card with the lowest interest rate.

4. Speaking of credit cards, now is a great time to examine your bills and see what kind of expenses you might be able to eliminate. If you're not paying off your balance each month, think about how you can work toward that goal.

5. Finally, get a free credit report each year to make sure you are aware of all your accounts and credit. Fixing any errors or issues in advance will come in handy the next time you apply for a loan, credit card, or rent an apartment.

DAY 6
COUPON LIKE A PRO

DAILY INSPIRATION

Congratulations, you're close to finishing your first week of the Money Diet! Today's Savings Subject covers a key strategy for saving money: couponing. You won't believe how much you can save at the grocery store and beyond with just a few hours of work.

Coupons are just one more way that the Money Diet puts you in control of your life. Most people today are weighed down by the rising cost of food, gas, and living expenses in general. It's hard for many of us to make ends meet. As you read this book, you should start to feel a difference in your attitude about money. If you start off frustrated about how hard it is to save, our hope is that chapter by chapter you will begin to feel empowered to make a change. Knowing that you're taking advantage of savings all around you should make you feel good! Stay empowered and remember that this is just one step in a journey to a better life.

WHO KNEW?   **QUICK TIP**

You can print out most internet coupons twice from one computer. Just click your internet browser's "back" button, or go back to the site's homepage and search for the coupon again so you can get the same savings twice!

Savings amount: The sky's the limit!

SAVINGS SUBJECT
Coupon Like a Pro

We'll admit it, we were never huge couponers. But after finding out how much you can save—and watching our friends walk out of the store with hundreds of dollars' worth of groceries for less than $20—we decided to give it a shot. It seems simple on the face of it: Hand over a coupon for a few cents off a product, then get that product at a discount. But with a few easy tips and hints, you can go from getting just a few cents off to getting all of your products at half off or more—and some things even for free! In this section, we'll tell you everything you need to know about couponing, whether you want to keep it casual or go extreme.

COUPON STRATEGIES

If you've never couponed or have only been a casual couponer, there are a few strategies you need to know. These bits of know-how will take you from saving just a few cents here or there to saving hundreds per month on your grocery bill.

- **Coupon stacking is okay.** Many novice coupon-clippers don't realize that it's almost always possible to use more than one coupon per item (called "stacking" coupons)—even if your coupon says "limit one." That's because most stores allow you to use a manufacturer coupon (like the kind that come in the Sunday paper) with a store coupon (like the kind that come in flyers from the store).
- **Buy more and save.** Also make sure to keep in mind that if you buy (for example) three jars of tomato sauce, you can use three coupons for that spaghetti sauce. Read on to find out some of our strategies for getting multiple coupons for the same item. Then stock up to save!
- **Combine coupons with sales.** Coupons can also be combined with in-store sales, and it's easy to find out what sales are going on at your local supermarket and which recent coupons can be used for the same objects. Simply type your grocery store's name and the phrase "coupon match-ups" into a search engine and find blogs that do all the work for you.
- **Buy what's on sale, use it later.** The biggest difference between extreme couponers and regular shoppers is that extreme couponers buy what's on sale, even if they don't need that item

at the moment. This is a smart strategy because you can get products at the lowest price possible, and then you'll have it when you need it. It's important to have a space in your home where you can store items that you've bought on sale—a few shelves in a basement or a storage closet works well.

- **Study your stores' policies.** Different stores have different coupon policies, so check at your store's customer service desk to find out if they place any restrictions on the types and amount of coupons you can use.

WHERE TO FIND COUPONS ONLINE

Looking for free, printable coupons online? Here are some of the best sites to find them. Sites with an asterisk (*) allow you to add coupons electronically to your store's loyalty card without having to print them out!

- **AllYou.com/coupons-deals**
- **CellFire.com***
- **CoolSavings.com/printable_coupons***
- **CouponNetwork.com***
- **Coupons.com***
- **MamboSprouts.com***
- **RedPlum.com***
- **SavingStar.com***
- **ShopAtHome.com**

- **Shortcuts.com***
- **SmartSource.com**
- **Ecoupons.upromise.com*** **(savings go into a college fund)**
- **Valpak.com**
- **WhoKnewTips.com/ExtremeCoupons**

WHO KNEW?　　　QUICK TIP

When asked for your zip code to print out online coupons, type in a few different zip codes to see what coupons crop up. You may have to log out and log back in again but it could help you find more savings.

WHERE TO FIND EVEN MORE COUPONS

Even with how easy online coupons can be, physical coupons—the old-fashioned kind that are already printed out, of course—are still a huge source of discounts and an essential part of any couponer's repertoire. Here's how to supercharge your coupon stockpile!

- **Scour your Sunday paper.** If you're interested in getting into couponing big-time, the insert from your paper's Sunday edition is a must. Many papers offer Sunday- or weekend-only subscriptions that will pay for themselves in coupon savings. Some weekends, your Sunday paper will have so many coupon inserts that it's worth it to get another paper! Plan ahead by visiting SundayCouponPreview.com, which will tell you what coupons are going to be offered in your upcoming Sunday paper.

- **Get coupons at the store.** While shopping, keep an eye out for coupons in the aisles. Many stores have blinking machines that offer coupons, or coupons on tear-pads that are attached to shelves. Take a few and save them for when that item is on sale! You may also want to check at the customer service desk and at the pharmacy.

- **Get the word out.** Make sure your coworkers, friends, relatives, and neighbors all know that you're a coupon-clipper, and ask them to save any coupon inserts they find. Perhaps it's their guilt about not taking advantage of coupons themselves, but you'll be surprised at how many extra coupons you'll receive from them! You can also trade coupons you don't need for those you do with couponing friends.

- **Create a source for coupons.** Want even more people to trade with? How about making a "Take a Coupon, Leave a Coupon" box? Set it up at your office, or ask your church, library, or a local cafe if you can place one there. Everyone leaves coupons they can't use, and takes what they can.

You'll love stopping by to see what you can get your hands on.

- **Trade online.** A "coupon train" is a group of couponers who send coupons they don't need to other couponers. Try Googling "coupon train" to find online groups that you can join!

- **Go straight to the source.** If there is a name-brand product you use regularly, but you can never seem to find coupons for it, try visiting the company's website for coupons. If it doesn't have any, see if you can find a customer service email address for the company and write to them to ask for coupons. This usually works best if you ask for coupons for a specific product, especially if it's brand new to the market.

WHEN TO BUY

With all the excitement of watching your coupons add up, you might begin to wonder, "When do I use my best coupons?" While having one coupon for an item is great, extreme couponers usually make sure they are getting the lowest possible price for an item by stacking up several coupons and a sale. Here are a few examples of prime moments for coupons:

- **Aim for an overage.** An "overage" is when the total value of your coupons is actually higher than the sale price of an item. Ding, ding, ding!

As if you needed us to tell you, overages are the *best* times to buy! Most stores will not give you actual cash back for overages, but some stores will give you a store credit. Otherwise, you'll have to buy more items (basically getting them for free) to cover the overage.

- **Take advantage of "buy one, get one free" sales.** These promotions are so exciting to deal-lovers that they have their own acronym: BOGO. The reason why they're so thrilling? Because you can usually use manufacturer coupons for the item you're getting for free! For instance, your CVS is having a BOGO sale on Pantene shampoo, and you found a 50¢ off coupon online. Print it out twice, then take both coupons to the store and use them to get $1 off your BOGO purchase!

- **Use coupons when prices are 50 percent or lower.** A good rule of thumb when you're beginning to coupon is to buy the item if you can get it for 50 percent off its usual price. If it's 75 percent off or more, consider it a bargain worthy of stockpiling!

- **Use right before expiration dates.** If you've been saving your coupons in an attempt to get a lower price on a particular item, but your coupons are about to expire, go for it now before it's too late. You may be able to get a better price later, but getting a few at the current discount price is never a bad idea, especially since it's more fun to be rewarded for your coupon-saving savvy.

WHO KNEW? **QUICK TIP**

Make sure to ask if the store where you're shopping accepts competitors' coupons. Many stores, such as The Home Depot and Lowe's, as well as most national office supply chains, will accept other stores' coupons! This will allow you to more easily stack coupons.

FINDING COUPONS AND REBATES FOR NONFOOD ITEMS

If you're looking for coupons for clothing, electronics, or other household items, you may have to go beyond the usual sources. Here are some places were you can find coupons for nonfood items.

- **Sign up for coupons.** Signing up for a store's credit card is a quick and easy way to make sure you receive their coupons in the mail, and most stores also offer extra perks to cardholders. Just make sure you aren't overdoing it—having lots of store credit cards can hurt your credit rating even if you regularly pay off the balance.

You can also see if the store has a mailing list you can sign up for.

- **Ask for coupons at the store.** Believe it or not, many stores—especially department stores—have coupons and rebates available just for the asking. You may not see them advertised, but if you go up to the customer service counter and ask for any current coupons, don't be surprised if you're handed some big savings!

- **Check the Yellow Pages.** The Yellow Pages are a great source of coupons, especially if you're looking for coupons on services like house cleaning or plumbing. Before you recycle your phone book, take a look to see if there's a special coupon section and skim the ads to see if there are any big coupons you may want to use.

- **Check your mall's website.** Did you know that the websites of many malls now offer coupons? If you're headed to the mall, check their site for exclusive coupons and links to the coupons offered by the websites of the various stores inside.

- **Get coupons at the post office.** Looking for coupons for big-ticket items for your home like washing machines, TVs, and more? Stop by your local post office and grab a packet for people who are moving and would like their mail forwarded. Even if you don't fill out the forwarding card, these packets often contain coupons from stores targeting those who have recently moved.

DAY 6
FINANCIAL FITNESS PLAN
Dealing with Collection Agencies and other Debt Collectors

We've all been there: the phone rings, you see it's an "unknown number," and you know it's a creditor calling. If you're like many people, you have so many creditors calling that you've begun to get overwhelmed. In this section we're going to help you get started in tackling these calls by filling you in on the options you have for paying off debt.

Before you start picking up those calls, take a look at any collection notices, as well as overdue statements, you collected on Day 3. Almost all collection agencies will allow you to sign up for a monthly payment plan, but make sure that the payment amount is sensible. Figure out how much you can afford to pay each month before you agree to a deal. The last thing you want to do is agree to a monthly payment amount that is out of your budget.

The first tactic of many collection agencies is to get you to pay the total amount due. Don't feel forced to do this. Most collection agencies will settle for 40–60 percent of the total amount owed. It's best to name your price and see if they find it agreeable. Whether they agree or not, remember that the person you're talking to is just doing his or her job. If you're polite during the entire call, he or she will be more likely to help you out. Whatever you do, don't lose your cool.

If a collection agency has been unable to show you proof that you owe the debt, threatens to take you to court when you ask for a payment plan or lowered settlement amount, or otherwise seems fishy, don't be afraid to go to court with the collection agency. Not only do you deserve to tell your side of the story to a neutral arbitrator, but cases brought by collection agencies have been overturned in many state and local courts. Just make sure you stay apprised of court dates and show up to every one of them. If you don't show up to make your case, the judge will have no choice but to side with the collection agency.

Once you've agreed to a monthly payment amount, set up a direct debit or other way to remind yourself to make payments. If you've agreed to a lower rate it may be stipulated that all of your payments must be made on time. Mark due dates on your calendar and pat yourself on the back for dealing with your debt head-on.

DAY 7
SHOPPING SECRETS REVEALED

DAILY INSPIRATION

On Day 7, we go shopping! First, we'll hit the stores, showing you how to make your dollar go further on clothes, computers, and more. Plus, we'll learn *when* to look for the best deals, whether it's January deals on discounted oatmeal or May deals on car wash supplies. Then we head online to show you some of our favorite tricks for navigating web deals so that you can be a smarter internet shopper.

It finally happened. You were doing great with cutting costs and freeing up extra money to pay down your debt. Then you went shopping with a friend, tried on a must-have dress, and poof: $200 just disappeared. Or maybe you couldn't say no to going in with your buddies on season tickets for your favorite sports team. Any way you look at it, you're back in the hole. Take a moment and be patient with yourself. It's a learning process. There's an old Japanese proverb that says if you fall down seven times, you should get back up eight. Think of all the progress you've made, and keep going despite the setbacks!

DAILY SAVINGS SUBJECT
Shopping Secrets Revealed

Earn money for internet searches. With Bing Rewards (Bing. com/rewards), you can earn credits toward online gift cards by using Bing as a search engine.

SHOP TILL YOU SAVE

Shopping can be a lot of fun, but it can also get us in a lot of trouble. Try these suggestions for saving money when you head out to the stores.

- **Decode the clearance section.** Have you ever noticed that the clearance section is always at the back of the store? It's because the store wants you to walk past all the tempting full-priced merchandise first. Once you finally make your way to the sale rack, you've probably noticed that it's usually a mess. That's intentional, too; it's designed to frustrate you, so that you gravitate toward the newer, neatly organized items. Once you understand this strategy, you can stop falling for it. Ignore the neat stuff and muddle through the mess for the best savings. ***SAVINGS AMOUNT: 20-90 PERCENT OFF ORIGINAL RETAIL PRICE.***

- **Be loud, be proud, be thrifty!** Many people are intimidated by shopping at thrift shops. How do you know you're getting something good? What should you be wary of? First of all, it's easier than you might think to find good quality second-hand clothes. If the clothes seem dingy or dirty, find a different shop. Many resale shops are organized by the color of the clothing, but most also use some kind of color-coded tag system (so that all items with a red tag are 50 percent off, for instance). Best of all, you can usually exchange your clothes for money or store credit. Make sure to ask if the store offers you more "money" for your item if you opt for credit rather than cash. And have fun looking for bargains! You never know what fantastic find you're going to get. (P.S. Try visiting wealthier neighborhoods for the best finds. Not only do the wealthy shop at these stores less often—leaving more goodies for you—they often have nicer things to give away!) **SAVINGS AMOUNT: 50-90 PERCENT OFF ORIGINAL RETAIL PRICE.**

- **Buy at auction.** Every month, hundreds of cars and other merchandise are confiscated by the police. And hey, just because a criminal used it, it doesn't make that $100 laptop any less useful. Look in the classifieds section of your newspaper to find local auctions, or check out PropertyRoom.com or PoliceAuctions.com to find unbelievable deals on tools, electronics, bicycles, video games, and more.

- **Spend where it counts.** Buy most of your basics—solid-color shirts, white blouses, socks, black dresses, and so forth—at the cheaper stores. Save the expensive stores for the uniquely designed and patterned clothes, where you can see the difference in quality.

- **Befriend those in the know.** If you have a favorite shop you find yourself spending a lot of time in, make sure to get friendly with the sales staff. Clothing stores often have unannounced sales, but if you're friendly with the people who work there, they'll often tip you off. And if they really like you, they may let you put an item on layaway until it goes on sale a few days later.

SHOP SEASONALLY FOR SAVINGS

Sales cycles vary from store to store, which is why you have to keep track of your own store's cycle to see the most savings. But there are some seasonal sales you can count on to happen each year in the U.S. Here they are, broken down by month:

January. Post-holiday grocery store items like candy, turkey, ham, and stuffing; diet foods like low-calorie frozen meals and snacks; oatmeal (It's National Oatmeal Month, believe it or not); Super Bowl foods like chips and soda.

February. Dog food; waffles; condoms and other family planning products (before Valentine's Day); candy (after Valentine's Day); canned vegetables and tuna.

March. Frozen foods including pizza and ice cream;

cleaning products; paper products like paper towels and plates; Cajun seasonings and mixes (in celebration of Mardi Gras).

WHO KNEW? QUICK TIP

Shop at stores that match or beat their competitors' advertised prices and those that offer price adjustments. That way, you'll eliminate the buyer's remorse that comes when an item you purchased goes on sale a week later.

April. After-Easter items such as baking supplies, candy, ham, and eggs; Earth Day items like reusable tote bags and organic foods; olive oil; butter; post-Passover items like matzo, potatoes, and coconut flakes.

May. Pet food, treats, and toys; sunscreen and bug spray; picnic items like condiments (ketchup, barbecue sauce, etc.), hot dogs, ground beef, soda, buns, and plastic forks; Cinco de Mayo promotions like salsa, tortillas, and taco shells; car wash and maintenance items.

June. Dairy products; produce; salad dressing; pre-Fourth of July sales on charcoal and other supplies.

July. Post–Fourth of July sales on charcoal, hot dogs, ground beef, buns, and picnic supplies; produce; bottled water and soda; school supplies.

August. Cleaning items; dorm room and school supplies; lunch meat, Jell-O cups, and other lunch-box essentials; produce; kids' summer toys, as well as fans, pool-cleaning equipment, and anything else summer-related.

September. Cereal; canned goods (especially tomato products); baby products; produce.

October. Seafood; pie shells and filling; premade foods like macaroni and cheese and pizza; dog food; produce; safety equipment like smoke alarms.

November. Candy; baking products including chocolate chips, cake mixes, and nuts; coffee and tea; soup and broth; Thanksgiving foods like stuffing, instant potatoes, and gravy mix.

December. Baking products; pasta and tomato sauce; turkeys (after Thanksgiving and Christmas); crackers; canned goods; oranges and grapefruit; toys; cold remedies and other medicine; toothbrushes; vitamins.

You're shopping in your favorite store and notice that there are tons of markdowns. After you fill your arms with bargains, go home and mark the day on your calendar! Most stores receive shipments of new goods every 9–12 weeks and discount current merchandise to make room for the new stuff. Return to the store during that time frame to find more deals. *Savings amount: 15–50 percent per shopping trip.*

ONLINE SAVINGS

Every year, the percentage of people shopping online increases. And why not? The internet is a fantastic place to save money, as long as you know where to look. Plus, online shopping is great for those of us with busy lifestyles who don't have time to get to the mall or the big-box discount stores. Here are some of our favorite sites and tips for finding deals on the web:

- **First stop for online shopping.** Use PriceGrabber. If you're looking for deals online, check out PriceGrabber.com. It lets you see what's on sale in various categories, then takes you right to the site to get the bargain. Best of all, you can see the prices at different sites side by side, including sales tax and shipping! It's also a great resource for finding hundreds of active manufacturers' rebates, including links to the rebate forms online.

- **Ibotta bargain!** Ibotta is a free iPhone app that helps you get cash back for the products you buy every day. It works at a handful of major stores like Walmart, Target, and Walgreens. You answer some questions, watch a short video or learn about different products, and then upload a picture of the receipt showing that you bought it. ***SAVINGS AMOUNT: $1-$20 PER SHOPPING TRIP.***

- **Scan for savings.** If you own an iPhone, Android, or other smartphone, you have access to applications that make shopping less expensive. Search your phone's app store for Barcode Scanner on iPhone and Android, ScanLife on Blackberry, and ShopSavvy for Windows phones. Once the applications are installed, you can use your phone's camera to take a snapshot of the barcode, or enter the UPC numbers underneath. Your phone will then give you a list of how much the item costs at locations near you and online. If you don't have a smartphone, you can still easily compare prices online by using Google's Product Search (Products.Google.com).

Just type in the numbers found near the bar-code and away you go!

- **Get great clothing on clearance.** At ShopIt-ToMe.com, you enter your favorite brands of clothes and they do all the online searching for you. When items come up for sale on a department store's site, they'll send you an email, alerting you of the discount. The best part is, you can specify your size, so you won't have to waste your time wading through links only to find that the store is all out of extra-large!

WHO KNEW?   QUICK TIP

Companies are more likely to offer coupons to new customers in the hopes of enticing them to buy. Before you shop online, try clearing your internet browser's cookies (your Help menu will usually tell you how). These cookies tell the site that you've been there before, so if you clear them they may think you're a new customer!

Savings amount: The sky's the limit!

DAY 7
FINANCIAL FITNESS PLAN
Do You Overspend? Here's How to Get It Under Control

Today we'll look at the reasons why you always spend an extra $25 at the grocery store or why you can't resist picking up a new top that you don't need to go along with the new jeans that you do. We'll also offer suggestions for how to deal with those impulses and keep yourself on the path to financial fitness.

- **Paying with credit.** When you use a credit card to pay for purchases, you don't feel the immediate financial impact because there's a grace period between when you spend the money and when you actually have to fork it over. With plastic, it's much easier to throw a few extra items into the grocery cart or to order that extra appetizer or glass of wine while dining out. Try switching over to cash. If you only have a certain dollar amount in your wallet, you'll be forced to stay on budget.

- **"But it was on sale!"** Sales can be irresistible, but they can also lead to overspending. You may find yourself browsing the sale section of your favorite clothing website and end up buying three items instead of one just because the store is advertising a one-day promo of 25 percent off the already discounted sale prices. You think to yourself: Who knows when such a great deal will come around again? When you start to feel like this, step back for a moment and ask yourself: Is this the kind of item you'd buy even if it weren't on sale? Do you absolutely need this item? If the answer is no, think twice before going forward with the purchase.

- **Falling for store tricks.** In this chapter, we've shown you some of the tricks stores use to keep you away from the clearance section. In addition, experts have shown that the type of music a store plays can cause you to spend more. The same is true for store-specific smells. It can be as obvious as the cologne wafting from an Abercrombie and Fitch to subtler fragrances that you can barely notice. Finally, you should know that most customers move through a store from right to left, so merchandisers will place their newest, priciest items there. Once you understand a little bit about the psychology of retailing, you can stop falling into the tempting traps laid out for you.

- **Shopping without a list.** When you head to the supermarket, be sure to go with a list in hand. If you don't, you're more likely to throw anything appealing in your cart. First, sit down and think about what you'd like to eat for the week and then write down all of the items you need to prepare those dishes. You'll not only save money by sticking to the list, but you'll also be less likely to waste food.

- **Shopping makes you feel better.** A little "retail therapy" is OK now and again, but if you make a habit of splurging every time you have a bad day—or a good day—you can soon find yourself in financial trouble. Shopping can give you a short-term high, but it can't solve your problems. The next time you want to reach for the plastic, try calling a friend or taking a walk instead.

DAY 8
SAVE ON WATER AND ELECTRICITY

DAILY INSPIRATION

Today you learn savings strategies that benefit your wallet *and* the planet. Conserving water and electricity can significantly reduce your monthly bills while giving you the pride that comes from being an eco-warrior! It's time to step up your money diet with bold moves like investing in a SmartStrip (read on to know more) and becoming an energy-sparing night owl. Your budget and our delicate Earth will thank you.

Congratulations! You have finished your first week of the Money Diet and you've already made some positive changes. You may have even saved some serious money. Tally up all the Savings amounts from the tips you've used or plan to use and write that number down somewhere you can see it every day. Today is a good day to reward yourself for being a successful saver: Take a nice, long walk (it's free!). Revel in nature's bounty or the city's splendor and just breathe. Your lungs, legs, and soul will thank you for it. Enjoy this new sense of accomplishment that comes from making small improvements in spending and resolve to make it part of your everyday life.

SAVING SUBJECT
Save on Water and Electricity

The United States Department of Energy estimates that American households spend about $1,900 a year on energy costs. Master the forces of electricity and water, and the savings will be noticeable! You don't have to practice all of the following advice at once. Take advantage of these pointers little by little until you start to see the savings in your monthly bills. Nothing motivates like progress.

ELECTRIC BILLS: NO MORE JUICE ON THE LOOSE

- **Unplug.** Your appliances are 24/7 energy suckers as long as they're connected to an outlet. So when you're not using the blender, toaster, food processor or television, pull the plug. Of course, appliances that need constant power to maintain a setting should stay on. *ANNUAL SAVINGS: $190.*

- **Get smart.** Smart Power strips go beyond old-fashioned surge protecting. They reduce the amount of electricity you use by cutting off power when a plugged-in device is not in use. And the strips cut power to related devices when appropriate. For example, when you shut off your desktop computer, the strip will cut the power to the printer, scanner, and monitor, too. The Environmental Protection Agency says a few Smart Strips will pay for themselves in a couple of months. *ANNUAL SAVINGS: $100.*
- **Put appliances on the night shift.** Keep the homemaking hours of an owl and save big. The price of electricity and other utilities often goes down at night, making it the right time to run the washing machine and dishwasher. Most electric companies charge more for power usage during the day. Contact your local utility to find out if that's the case in your area. You can expect to take a 10 to 15 percent bite out of your power bill. *ANNUAL SAVINGS: $200 OR MORE.*
- **Apply for an energy-budget boost.** The US government's Low Income Home Energy Assistance Program (LIHEAP) helps pay for heating, electricity, and sometimes even cooling costs for your home. You can enroll in the program whether you rent or own, and you don't

necessarily need to be receiving other government assistance to qualify. Each state's program is different, so for more information, do an internet search for "energy assistance" and your state's name.

RUNNING THE REFRIGERATOR

It costs about $120 a year to run your refrigerator and freezer. See if you can chip away at some of that cost and keep a little extra in your wallet.

- **Clean the fridge door.** If your refrigerator is more than a couple of years old, its seal is probably not as tight as it used to be. To save energy and keep your food cooler, first clean the door's gasket (that rubber lining that goes around it), then rub it with petroleum jelly to ensure a tighter seal.

- **Test the seal for leaks.** If cleaning and lubricating the rubber lining that runs around the door (also known as the gasket) doesn't work, the gasket could be loose. To find out, close the door on a piece of paper. If you can pull it out without it ripping, your gasket is indeed loose. To figure out where, turn on a battery-powered lamp or flashlight and place it in your fridge. Turn the lights off in your kitchen and close the door. Wherever you see light peeking through, cold air is leaking! Try re-gluing your gasket or buying a new one from wherever you purchased your fridge.

WHO KNEW?   **QUICK TIP**

Buying a new refrigerator can actually save you money over time! Today's Energy Star-certified models are much more efficient when compared to fridges made before 1990.
Savings amount: $100 a year.

- **Put a lid on it.** You can make your refrigerator more energy efficient by understanding how it works. Refrigerators use energy to reduce the humidity inside, which helps cool foods. Therefore, any time you leave an open container of liquid inside, you're wasting energy. Make sure all your pitchers have lids, and make sure dressings and moist leftovers are well covered. You should also let hot foods cool before placing them in the refrigerator, so the fridge doesn't have to use extra energy to bring them down to room temperature. Of course, be careful with cooked meats, eggs, and poultry—they shouldn't stay out of the refrigerator for more than an hour.
- **Keep freezer full.** Your freezer is more energy efficient when it's full, so don't be shy about

stuffing it as much as possible. When you're running low on food items, just fill a few empty juice cartons or soda bottles with water and use them to fill up the space.

- **Move heat sources.** It may be time to rearrange your kitchen for energy-efficient savings. Keeping appliances that heat things up (like a stove, oven, or toaster) away from your refrigerator will make it easier for your fridge and freezer to stay cold, which can save you lots of money in the long run.

WATER SAVINGS

Water bills are rising along with all the other utility bills, but with these methods for regulating your water usage you should see some relief.

WHO KNEW?   **QUICK TIP**

Cut back on the amount of space you take up in your dishwasher and save on water costs by washing large pots and pans the old-fashioned way—in the sink. Even if you use a little extra water to wash these items separately, you'll save a lot of water in fewer loads washed.

- **Turn off the faucet.** Every minute you spend brushing your teeth or shaving with the water running, you're wasting up to three gallons. The average family of four squanders 6,000 gallons a year on brushing alone. That's about 14 hot tubs full. Be sure to run the faucet only when you're using the water. ***ANNUAL SAVINGS: $70.***

- **Stop the gushers.** Pay attention to other water wasters. Use a bucket of soapy water to wash the car and resort to the hose only for a quick rinse. You'll save 90 gallons of water per car. Likewise, make sure that washing machines and dishwashers are full before doing a load.

- **Install aerators.** The easiest way to lower your water usage (and utility bill) is to screw low-flow aerators into your faucets. Aerators are easy to install, cost a dollar or less, and can save you a nice chunk of change every year. ***ANNUAL SAVINGS: $50 OR MORE.***

- **Mark the water setting.** Quit fiddling with the knobs on your shower when trying to get the water just right before you hop in. Find your favorite setting, then mark where the knob is pointing on the tile with a dab of nail polish. This water-preserving trick is great for kids, who often take a long time adjusting the water before they get in.

- **Enforce shorter showers.** If you have teenagers, try giving them an incentive to take shorter showers. A great one is five minutes added on to their curfew for every minute they shave off their showering time.

WHO KNEW?   QUICK TIP

The average monthly water bill is $50. If the showerheads in your home were installed before 1994, you should seriously consider replacing them with their modern, energy-saving equivalents. Check out your local hardware store for low-flow alternatives, and remember that just because it's low-flow doesn't mean it has to be weak!

Annual savings: $300.

TOILET TRAINING: STAYING FLUSH WITH CASH

- **Keep a bottle in the tank.** Remember the old trick of placing a brick in your toilet tank to save water? Right idea, wrong implement. Try a two-liter water bottle filled with water instead. Every time you flush, you can conserve between a half-gallon to gallon of water, or up to about 10 gallons a day in a typical home, according to The Daily Green. But if you must use a brick, go ahead. Just make sure to seal it in a plastic bag. *ANNUAL SAVINGS: $100.*

- **Check for leaks.** Does your toilet have a leak? To find out, put a drop of food coloring in the tank and see if it shows up in the bowl. If it does, fix the leak to save up to 73,000 gallons of water per year!

THE LAUNDRY LIST

Laundry costs may not be something you think about, but when you consider the amount of water and electricity you must use every week getting every last sock in your house clean and dry it's not hard to believe that there's money to be saved.

- **Dry similar fabrics together.** Dry light-weight items like T-shirts and underwear in one load and heavier items like denim and towels immediately after for faster dry times. Doing back-to-back loads in the dryer allows you to take advantage of leftover heat from the previous cycle.

- **Dry al fresco.** Line drying your clothes is energy efficient and great for them. Not only is air-drying less harsh, you'll love the real smell of sun-dried linens. If you don't have a clothesline, hang shirts and pants on hangers from tree limbs! Just make sure not to put brights in the sun, as they may fade.

- **Clean the lint screen.** Removing the lint from the screen in your dryer may not be enough to make sure it is running as efficiently as possible. The fabric softener used in dryer sheets can get caught in the mesh, even if you can't see it. To be sure you're completely cleaning the screen, remove it and clean it with warm, soapy water and a brush. Leave it out to dry completely before placing back in your dryer.
- **Wash in cold.** No spin needed here. If you wash your clothes in cold water, you will save. Try Tide 2X Ultra for Cold Water. *Consumer Reports* ranked it first in erasing the toughest stains, including grass and wine. ***ANNUAL SAVINGS: $60.***

WHO KNEW? QUICK TIP

Takes clothes for another spin. If you find your clothes are still dripping wet when you take them out of the washing machine, put them back in and set the cycle to spin. The extra spin time will wring them out even further, and use less energy than extra time in the dryer will.

THE DISH ON DISHWASHERS

Check out these useful tips for keeping your dishwasher working as efficiently as possible:

- **Stop pre-rinsing.** Don't rinse the dishes before putting them in the dishwasher. You waste effort, *Consumer Reports* says, and you waste 6,500 gallons of water per year. Let the dishwasher alone wash the dishes. ***ANNUAL SAVINGS: $75.***

- **Turn off the dry cycle.** Much of the energy your dishwasher uses is during the dry cycle, when it heats up water to the point of steam. To save energy, turn off the dry cycle (or simply open your dishwasher after the rinse cycle is done). Leave the door open a crack and let your dishes drip-dry. You'll save a lot by avoiding the heat-drying cycle on your machine, and your glasses will streak less.

- **Pre-spray the dirtiest dishes.** Keep a spray bottle filled with water and a bit of dishwasher detergent near your dishwasher. If a dish is heavily soiled, spray it down before you put it inside. The detergent gets working on the food immediately, so you won't have to rinse your dishes before putting them inside, or run a separate "rinse" cycle before you do your dishes.

If you've ever turned a sprinkler or soaker hose on and have forgotten about it, then the mechanical water timer is the gadget for you. Available at your local hardware store, these hose attachments work like egg timers and turn off the water supply after the amount of time you specify, usually between 10 minutes and two hours.

GET MORE LIGHT FOR LESS

Did you know that paint color can help you heat your house? Read on for more.

- **Lighten up on the color.** If you're trying to decide between deep or baby blue for your walls, you should know that lighter colors of paint will help you use less energy. They reflect the light and heat in a room better than darker hues. Painting the outside of your house (and especially your roof) a light color also helps reflect light, which reduces the retention of heat and will keep your house cooler. *ANNUAL SAVINGS: $180.*

- **Go fluorescent.** See the light—change your bulbs to CFLs. Installing compact fluorescent bulbs in your house will brighten your budget more than you think. They last ten times longer using up to 75 percent less energy.

- **Be a turn-off.** It is one of the more obvious tactics but one of the easiest to ignore. Turn out the lights! Better yet, buy motion-activated lights—especially for bathrooms and hallways. They'll pay for themselves soon enough.

WATER HEATER

You may not think about your water heater much, but it might be time to start paying it some attention. Follow these suggestions and it will serve you much better:

- **Turn down your water heater.** You never use your water on full-blast when it's hot anyway, so it's worth it to decrease the maximum temperature. You can save up to $125 per year by simply lowering the thermostat on your hot water heater from 140° to 120° F. *ANNUAL SAVINGS: $125.*

- **Wrap it in a jacket.** A water heater insulation jacket (also called a blanket) costs $15–$35, but it can cut the cost to heat your water dramatically. By insulating your water heater, you'll cut down on the amount of energy it needs to heat standing water in half, also cutting down on the amount you need to pay. To find out if you need a water heater jacket, touch the side of your water heater. If it's warm, it's leaking energy.

- **Drain dirt buildup.** Make sure to drain your water heater once a year to get rid of sediment. Left too long, this grit can build up until you're using energy to heat sludge. To find out how to complete this simple home maintenance trick, type "how to drain a water heater" into Google or another search engine. And start to save!

DAY 8
FINANCIAL FITNESS
Create Your Budget

You're finally ready to create your budget. The best way to design a budget is to keep track of your spending for three to six months before creating it. Why so much time? If you only use one month's worth of expenditures the number will likely be too high or too low, as your spending fluctuates from month-to-month. It's best to track your spending for several months and then take the average amount and make that your budget. Don't worry if you over- or underfund certain categories at first, or completely forget a category altogether! You'll refine the details over several months, until you come to the right budget for you. Some categories to keep in mind as you begin are:

- **Mortgage/rent**
- **Homeowner's/renter's insurance**
- **Real estate taxes**
- **Home repairs**
- **Electricity**

- **Water**
- **Gas**
- **Cable**
- **Internet**
- **Cell phone and/or landline phone**
- **Groceries/Food**
- **Household products/cleaning supplies**
- **Toiletries/personal hygiene**
- **Car payment**
- **Gas**
- **Auto insurance**
- **Car repairs**
- **Emergency fund**
- **Retirement fund**
- **College, house, car, baby, or other fund**

Your budget should detail expenses for basic needs and should not include things like enhanced cell phone service or cable TV. If you have a lot of debt, make sure you are including your debt payments as necessities. After you determine how much you're spending on necessities, divide your remaining spending categories into needs, wants, and luxury items.

When budgeting, it's important to keep track of your cash. Avoid spending in cash whenever possible and opt instead to buy even small items, like a coffee, with a credit card. You may feel silly but this will allow you to track all your spending without having to write it down: the credit card statement will keep the log for you and you'll be able to account for all your expenditures. Eventually, when you know how much money you can spend on things like coffee runs, you can take out enough cash each week to cover those costs. But for now, use a card for most things to make balancing your budget easier. If you do buy in cash, keep your receipts in an envelope conveniently placed in your car or purse, and, daily, input them or write them on a spreadsheet.

Finally, a good way to come up with a fair budget is to first write down what you think you spend, then compare it to what you actually spend. Determine where you can make compromises and slash expenses so you can begin paying off your debt, saving for future goals, and relieving yourself of added stress.

DAY 9

SAVE ON HEATING AND COOLING COSTS

DAILY INSPIRATION

Congratulations in advance on cutting your heating and cooling bills. More power to you! You are on your way to reversing self-defeating money habits. But sometimes we all need some help. If debt is overwhelming you, consider the buddy system. An "accountability partner" is a great way to get support along the way.

Find someone in the same boat and as committed as you are to getting out of debt. Make yourselves available by phone and plan to meet once a month over coffee to discuss your progress. Avoid the temptation to recruit a family member or someone else close to you. They may lack the objectivity you need to get real feedback. By the same token, you might also be reluctant to tell your debt buddy the cold hard truths about their debt management. Remember this: When it comes to conquering debt, nothing should be unsaid. Sometimes it takes a friendly ear to get you to be willing to utter the not-so-friendly truth.

DAILY SAVINGS SUBJECT
Save on Heating and Cooling Costs

So you want to save big on energy bills? In this chapter we're going right to the source. Heating and cooling your home sucks up 40 percent of your energy budget each month. Tame that, and your financial fitness will start reaching its potential. The seasonal extremes wreak the most havoc on your checkbook. In the winter, for instance, warm air rises and escapes through holes and gaps toward your home's upper reaches. In comes the colder air from below, creating a drafty nightmare. Even new homes aren't immune to uncomfortable swings in temperature. Just because a house meets the building code doesn't mean it's up to standards for ideal energy efficiency. Follow these tips to stay warm and cool on the cheap.

MIND THE VENTS

It's easy to forget about the vents in your home, but remembering them can mean added savings.

WHO KNEW?   **QUICK TIP**

Invest now to save later. Sealing leaky or badly insulated ducts that track through attics or crawl spaces can save you money in the long run, according to RehabAdvisor.com. The $500 you pay to get them fixed could save you thousands over time. *Annual savings: $400.*

- **Close the vents.** Close the heating and air-conditioning vents in rooms in your home you don't frequently use, like a guest room or laundry room. If your vents don't have closures, simply seal them off with duct tape.
- **Clean the vents.** Make sure to vacuum your heating and air conditioning vents regularly. When they get caked up with dust, your furnace or air conditioner has to work much harder! For the best energy efficiency, make sure to keep them dust-free.

SEAL UP FOR SUPER SAVINGS

Feel a draft in your wallet? That's money fluttering away due to too many unplugged openings and too little insulation. Sealing leaks and beefing up insulation can make your home 20 percent more energy efficient and knock 10 percent off your energy bill, according to the EPA.

- **Caulk any leaks.** Just follow the air and you'll find most leaks in the basement or attic around wiring entryways, ducts, and plumbing vents. A caulking gun can sometimes be enough to do the trick. Internet help is available at EnergyStar.gov or by Googling "plug leaks."
- **Seal electrical outlets.** Did you know that you could be losing warm (or cold) air through your electrical outlets? We placed some fireproof foam insulation under our outlet covers and switch plates and saved several dollars a month on our utility bill.
- **Winterize your door.** If you have a sliding glass door that's rarely used during the winter, seal the top, bottom, and sides with duct tape to keep cold air from coming in.

WHO KNEW?   QUICK TIP

Solar power your house: When the heat's on, open the blinds on windows that are exposed to the sun. When you have the AC going, close as many blinds as possible.

THERMOSTATS

Thermostats are a budget management tool at your fingertips. Use them wisely and you can save big:

- **Turn down the thermostat.** What may seem like an obvious move is sometimes ignored. But the cost relief is immediate without much sacrifice. You will save between 1 and 3 percent on your heating bill for every degree you lower the thermostat, according to TheDailyGreen.com.

- **Place thermostats away from the heat.** For accurate temperature readings, make sure to place your thermostat away from sources of artificial heat, such as ovens, appliances, computers, or direct sunlight. An inaccurately high temperature at the thermostat will cause the rest of the house to be colder than you want it to be. Similarly, make sure that cold air, such as that from windows or wiring holes, isn't making its way to the thermostat either. Also, ensure your thermostat is reading the inside room temperature and not the outside temperature.

- **Clean the thermostat.** If your furnace and AC don't seem to be paying attention to your thermostat, don't call the expensive repairman just yet. It could be a simple case of your thermostat's connectors being dirty. Take off the casing and run the point of an index card through the connectors to remove any crud. Stand back and cross your fingers, and your thermostat may be as good as new.

- **Install a programmable thermostat.** No sense in keeping up the heat if no one's home to enjoy it, right? A programmable thermostat can be set to reduce the temperature when the house is unoccupied. Very cool. ***ANNUAL SAVINGS: $180.***

KEEPING IT COOL

There are plenty of ways to maintain a cool home without wasting good money:

- **Close the closet doors.** In the summer months, make sure to keep your closet doors closed. Otherwise, you're paying to cool your closets, which will increase your energy bill.
- **Plant a tree.** One way we save money on our electric bill is by providing our house with natural shade. Planting trees and shrubs so that they shade the sunny side of your home will help cut down on the amount of air conditioning needed.
- **Go elsewhere for cool air.** Your local library may become more interesting than ever before with the air conditioning pumping through the stacks! Even spending a little bit of money at a coffee shop can be less expensive than running

your AC. If you have kids, going to an afternoon movie matinee can be a fun and frugal way to beat the heat.

FANS

If you don't have air conditioning or are trying not to use it to save money, invest in a few good fans, which will help disperse the cool air you do have and make it feel less warm because of the breeze.

Make a breezeway. If possible, make sure there's a pathway for the air to flow into and then out of your home—for example, from a window at the front of your house through to a window in the back—and use your fans to help aid this "breezeway." By doing this, you won't need to buy expensive oscillating fans or fans on a stand. Just get a few sturdy box fans and use them strategically!

- **Team up fans with AC.** It may feel like a waste to keep the fans on at the same time as the air-conditioner, but it's not. You'll actually save money, because you can keep the thermostat higher once you've created an internal breeze that will make you feel several degrees cooler (think of how much the wind outside affects how cool you feel, regardless of the actual temperature). For maximum energy efficiency, keep the fan on only while people are in the room.

- **Reverse ceiling fans for warmth.** Don't let your fan go to waste just because it's no longer warm outside. To stay toasty during the frigid days of winter, hit the reverse switch to push hot air down into your room.

WHO KNEW?   QUICK TIP

In the winter, don't just keep windows closed; make sure they're locked for the tightest possible seal. This could greatly reduce drafts.

KEEPING THE HEAT IN

Don't let your money leak out with the warm air. Use these tips to ensure that you're not over-paying for heat.

- **Reflect radiator heat.** Wrap a very large piece of corrugated cardboard in aluminum foil (shiny side out), and place it behind your free-standing radiator. The foil will reflect the heat, and you won't have to keep telling your landlord to turn up the boiler.
- **Let heat take its time.** When it's time to turn on the heat, be patient. Your house won't heat up any faster if you crank the thermostat way up, but you *are* likely to forget to turn it down, which can be a huge energy waster.

- **Wear a heavy sweater.** Simple but true. A light long-sleeved sweater adds about 2 degrees in warmth, while a heavy sweater tacks on about 4 degrees, according to the TheDailyGreen.com.
- **Try a fuel co-op.** A fuel co-op is an organization that negotiates lower rates for your heating gas by buying in bulk. Even though you normally have to pay a membership fee, you can save big bucks on your heating bill by joining a fuel co-op, and you often don't even need to change from your current gas company. Most co-ops will offer you discounts if you're a senior citizen or are on a fixed income. To find one in your region simply type "fuel co-op" and your geographic location into Google.

WHO KNEW?   **QUICK TIP**

It's true that it's not the heat that makes you feel warm: It's the humidity. Humid air feels warmer than dry air, so instead of cranking up the heat in the winter, run a humidifier. This allows you to turn down the heat, save energy, and still feel comfortable. Live, leafy plants also help raise humidity levels.

Monthly Savings: $50.

DAY 9
FINANCIAL FITNESS PLAN
Automatic Payment Systems

Automatic payment systems give you an opportunity to eliminate debt without thinking. It essentially turns any person into an efficient bill-paying machine. Today is the day to start using it if you haven't already. You will never pay another late fee, you'll save on postage, and your credit rating will be in better standing. Simply sign up with the company that's billing you for a service and the money will automatically go from your checking account direct to the company. The service is usually provided free by both the company and the bank, so it's all win-win, right?

Almost. You could hit trouble if you don't have sufficient funds in your account to support the withdrawals. Automatic means exactly that—the money continues to be withdrawn from your account like clockwork. Just make sure the money's there. You don't want to turn a smart move forward into a stumble backward with overdraft fees piling up. Keep your balance where it needs to be and automatic debits will work in your favor.

DAY 10
BUDGET-FRIENDLY BANKING

DAILY INSPIRATION

"Habit is habit and not to be flung out of the window by any man, but coaxed downstairs a step at a time." —Mark Twain

All of us have weak spots when we look honestly at our personal spending habits. For some it's eating out every weekend night; for others it's getting the latest technology as soon as it's debuted. It can be as big as home renovations that we don't need or as small as the daily latte on our way to work. Whatever pattern you're trying to break, be patient with yourself. One step at a time is the best way to break old habits.

A good first step is determining what triggers your desire to spend money. For many of us it's emotional. Tap in to the excuses you make to spend this money and you can begin to put that money towards your savings. Devising an action plan that suits you is another solid step toward breaking your bad spending habits. Maybe you'll resolve to make only one big change to your home every year or maybe you'll stop driving by that Starbucks every morning so you can resist temptation. It's not always easy to change, so give yourself time. We wish you luck as you take these steps in building better habits.

DAILY SAVINGS SUBJECT
Budget-Friendly Banking

LOWER YOUR INTEREST FEES AND BANK CHARGES

People who are in debt often sink deeper and deeper due to bank fees and high interest rates. The tips below will show you ways to lower or eliminate these fees and get more money in your bank account—not less!

BIG SAVER: ELIMINATE BANK FEES

If you're paying tons of money in fees to your bank, there are lots of things you can do about it! Check out our favorite tips below.

- **Switch banks.** It may be a pain, but if you're getting socked with fees for your checking or savings accounts, it's time to switch banks. You should never have to pay monthly service charges. Plus, many banks are now offering cash for opening a new account. Make sure to visit several banks in your area and ask about their fees, interest rates, opening bonuses, and other perks like free checking.

- **Find surcharge-free ATMs.** Sick of paying up to $3.81 (the average cost, according to Ally Bank) every time you have to visit an ATM? At AllPoint-Network.com, you can find all of the surcharge-free ATMs in your area by entering your city and state or your zip code. Many of the listings are for stores that offer cash-back with purchase, but you never know when you'll find a free ATM you never knew about. *SAVINGS AMOUNT: $2-$4 PER ATM USE.*

- **Get free checking, with interest.** At ING Direct, you never have to wait in line to see a teller—because they have no physical locations! Of course, if you're like us, you can't remember the last time you actually saw a teller anyway. The great thing about ING is that they not only offer free savings and CD accounts, but you can get an absolutely fee-free checking account that also gives you up to 1.24 percent interest! To put money into the account, set up direct deposit with your employer, or transfer money from other bank accounts for free. Visit INGDirect.com for more information and to open an account. *MONTHLY SAVINGS: $10–$25.*

- **Check for free checks.** The next time you're coming to the end of your box of checks, don't pay the bank for more. Instead, go to StylesChecks.com, where you can get a second box of checks for only 49 cents when you purchase your first box (just look for the link that says "Pricing" to see the special introductory offer). Also visit ChecksUnlimited.com/Introoffer.aspx, where you can get a free box of checks when you order three more boxes. ***SAVINGS AMOUNT: $9–$35.***

WHO KNEW?   QUICK TIP

Local and online banks often have the best deposit rates and lowest charges. You may not even have to leave your current bank. Some, like PerkStreet, can be linked to your existing accounts.

- **Join a credit union.** Tired of all the fees and high interest rates at your bank? Consider joining a federally insured credit union instead. These credit unions are not-for-profit (not to be confused with 'non-profit'), member-owned institutions. This allows them to be more beneficial for every account holder—not just the ultra-wealthy ones. We've also found that, if you need a loan, they are more open to discussing the possibilities with you, instead of denying you based solely on the numbers. To find one in your area and determine if it's right for you, visit NCUA.gov and select "Credit union data and application."

- **Stay on top of notices.** Read all communications you get from your bank, even those small slips that are included with your monthly statement (if you still get one in the mail) or announcements when you log on to your account online. A mailed notice may look like a promotion, but it might be a notification of new fees or restrictions. Read the fine print and call your bank to ask about anything that doesn't make sense. Also make sure to examine your bank statement every month for unexpected fees. If you're a longtime customer or have sizeable deposits, try to work out a better deal or ask to have certain fees waived.
- **Set up direct deposit to avoid fees.** In recent years, many banks, such as Chase, Bank of America, Citibank, and Wells Fargo have done away with their banking rewards and/or have imposed fees on checking accounts. But there are ways to avoid these fees. Fees are waived at many

banks if customers maintain a minimum balance or set up direct deposit with their employers. It's important to be aware of your bank's policies and if possible, meet the requirements to avoid extra fees.

- **Find out about hidden fees.** Many banks have begun to charge fees for things like simply using your debit card or visiting a teller. It's extremely important to be aware of the fees your bank charges and avoid accruing them. If you must do the things your bank charges for, it might be time to switch banks. Here are some fees we know about: Wells Fargo recently began a testing period of charging customers $3 to use their debit card in certain states; TD Bank and Bank of America e-banking customers are charged to get paper statements mailed to them; Bank of America charges $8.95 if a customer sees a teller for a deposit or withdrawal and PNC Bank charges $2–$3 if a customer transfers money via a service representative on the phone instead of doing it online; Bank of America now charges to replace a lost debit card. The more you know, the more you can save! *SAVINGS AMOUNT: $2–$8.95 PER TRANSACTION.*
- **Find free online checking.** Ally Bank offers a fee-free online checking account that pays

interest. Perkstreet Financial also has an online checking account that doesn't require a minimum balance and has no maintenance fees. *MONTHLY SAVINGS: $10–$25.*

WHO KNEW?   QUICK TIP

Debt consolidation is a smart and relatively painless way to ease some of the hardship. With debt consolidation, you can lower your monthly payments, and you may also be able to lock in a lower interest rate. The easiest kinds of consolidations to obtain are for student loans, but many banks also offer consolidation services for mortgages, and (if your credit score is good) credit card debt.

• **Close your account at the right time.** If you decide to switch banks, make sure you close your current account at the best time. Some banks charge for closing an account at certain times. For example, Chase charges $25 if you close an account within 90 days of opening it and PNC Bank and U.S. Bank charge $25 if you close an account within 180 days of opening it. You also want to ensure that any accrued but unpaid interest isn't lost. Modify the timing of your switch to minimize fees and maximize interest.

You can also check with your new bank to see if they offer a "switch kit," which can help simplify the process. **SAVINGS AMOUNT: $25.**

CREDIT CARD COMPREHENSION

Now that you have your bank account in order, it's time to lower your interest rates and get rid of other fees altogether on your credit cards. And of course, get on the road to paying off any balances!

- **Time for a transfer?** If you're thinking of getting a new or different credit card, keep an eye out for credit card offers in the mail in January and February. Companies usually offer their best deals (like a period of time with no interest payments) during the first six weeks of the year. If you have debt racked up from the holidays now is a perfect time to take advantage of balance transfer opportunities.

- **Split monthly payments in two.** Credit card interest is calculated based on your average daily balance over the month, which means you can reduce your charges by making more payments. Instead of paying, say, $300 at the end of the month, split that up into two $150 payments. That way, your average daily balance will be lower, and therefore your finance charges will be, too.

- **Transfer your balance.** If you owe lots of money to one credit card and not as much to one with a lower interest rate, ask your credit card company if you can do a balance transfer. You may incur a fee, but you often end up saving in the end. Many cards offer them for free during the first year of your agreement. If you have two cards from the same company, ask if the card with the better deal allows "credit reallocation," which would let you transfer not only the balance from the other card but its credit limit as well, without having to submit to another credit check.

WHO KNEW?   QUICK TIP

It sounds too simple to be true, but you can often just ask credit card companies, utilities, landlords, and others to waive late fees. If you're a longtime customer with a good history, companies will often re-credit your account, especially if it was your first offense. If you rack up two late fees every year, the money could really add up.

Annual Savings: $25–$50.

- **Ask for a lower APR.** If you want to reduce the annual percentage rate (APR) on your credit card, ask and you shall receive! It sounds too simple to be true, but one of the first things you should do when attempting to reduce your debt is call up your credit card company and ask them to reduce your interest rate or annual percentage rate. If you have had the card for a while and have routinely made payments on time, the company is usually happy to take this piece-of-cake step to keep your business.

- **Save the date.** There's an easy solution if you keep getting socked with late fees, or neglect to pay more than the minimum because the payment is due at the same time as your rent: Ask your credit card company to change the payment due date. It might take a few months to kick in, but you'll be able to pay down the card more easily at a time of the month when you're not strapped for cash. *MONTHLY SAVINGS: $25–$50.*

- **Get the best rewards for you.** These days, it's easy to get a credit card with some sort of reward program, so make sure you are getting something back for your spending, whether it's airline miles, hotel points, gas rewards, or good old cash back. Also check out cards that have low or no balance transfer fees and cards with low penalty or late fees if you have trouble paying your card on time. And if a card has an annual fee, determine if its rewards outweigh the fee.

- **Get more than rewards.** There are other benefits to certain credit cards aside from just rewards. Many cards offer roadside assistance, car rental insurance, or travel perks like waiving the fee of a checked bag, trip cancellation insurance, or access to exclusive airport lounges. Some cards offer purchase protections like return protection if a retailer won't accept your return, extended warranties, or theft insurance if an item is stolen within 30 days of purchase. Make your card work for you!

- **Awesome APR.** When getting a new card, it may seem that you want the card with the lowest APR, but make sure you read the fine print. Is the APR just introductory, and then it increases after six months? Is the rate variable or fixed? And just because a card has a low APR does not mean it's the best card for you, especially if you pay off your balance each month. Make sure you also look into the card's penalty and late fees, balance transfer fees, and foreign transaction fees if you travel a lot.

WHO KNEW?   QUICK TIP

Visit CreditCardNation.com to set up a calculator that estimates the time it will take to pay off your credit card debt when you enter in your total debt and how much you pay off each month.

- **Follow the golden rules.** It's easy to slip into credit card debt—don't let it happen to you! Only buy what you can afford with cash, pay off your balance every month to avoid high interest rates, and set a reminder each month to pay your bill to avoid late fees.
- **Friend your credit card.** "Like," "friend," or follow your credit card issuer on Facebook if you don't already. Many credit cards offer special perks and deals via Facebook, Foursquare, and Twitter. This can also make it easier to ask questions.

DAY 10
FINANCIAL FITNESS PLAN
When a Deal is Not a Deal

How many of us have bought something we really didn't need just because it was on sale or we had a coupon? If you wouldn't go to that store or use that service normally then it may not be such a bargain. Do you really need $50 in discounted cheese? Similarly, when you see an item you think you must have, put it on a wish list and check back in three days. Is it still a must-have? You'd be surprised at how many things lose their sparkle after a few days. Even if the item is on sale or part of some kind of deal, there's a good chance it will still be available. Plus, if you give yourself a few days or a week to think about it, you have time to cut money from other areas of your life to pay for the item!

Finally, a good way to curb spending is to make your credit card less available. Put it away for a period of time, and when you shop online never check the box that says "save this credit card information for future use." This feature makes it too easy to buy things impulsively when you're online shopping.

Remember, just because something seems like a "deal" doesn't mean you need to buy it!

DAY 11
PHONE, TV, AND INTERNET SAVINGS

DAILY INSPIRATION

Today we will discuss how you can lower your phone, TV and internet bills. But before we show you new ways to save, here's a great Day 11 project if you're in the mood: Consider making a visual debt reminder. The problem with debt is that it's invisible and easy to ignore. A visual reminder forces you to see your debt in a way that motivates you to fix it. Why not grab some markers and paper or poster board and get to work!

Start by making a list on a regular sheet of paper of all your debts, grouping them however it makes the most sense to you (smallest to largest, highest interest rate to lowest, etc.) and total the amount of everything you owe. Draw a large chart (use a poster board if you have it) showing your total debt in any way you want to represent it. The most important element of the visual reminder is the part that shows your progress. Make a thermometer-style debt chart where you fill in a line for every hundred dollars that you repay. Another approach is a giant progress bar chart detailing what you owe, how much you've paid and how much is left using different color markers. Some have even strung paper chains around their house representing their total debt with each link worth $100. The idea here is that every time you either pay or go below the amount on one of the links, you get to cut it off. Talk about a visually stimulating and satisfying way to keep your financial focus!

DAILY SAVINGS SUBJECT
Phone, TV, and Internet Savings

Unless you have sworn off all technological advances of this decade, choosing to communicate solely through the postal system, today's subject is a key component of your finances. You'd be surprised at all the money-saving possibilities that exist when you take the time to research them. Well, we've done the research for you. The tips listed in this section will streamline your phone, TV, and internet bills without forcing you to disconnect!

WHO KNEW?   QUICK TIP

Download some free apps at FreeAppADay.com. This is our favorite site for free apps offered for iPhone, iPad, and Android. Featured apps change daily, so make sure to sign up for their email alerts or follow them on Facebook and/or Twitter!

Savings amount: $0.99–$4 per application.

KEEP YOUR PHONE BILLS UNDER CONTROL

We are a nation of talkers. If you're chatting and texting on your cell phone as much as we are, you could very likely have an out-of-control cell phone bill. Sometimes all it takes is simply calling your cell service provider and asking nicely if they can lower your monthly rates. When you do make this call, state the facts—maybe your friend down the street with the same service plan is receiving a better price than you—and they might shave some dollars off your bill. Read on for more ways to trim your rising phone bill expenses.

- **Check if you qualify for a free cell phone plan.** You may have heard of the national "Lifeline Across America" phone program to help those who can't afford phone service. Did you know that this service is now available for cell phone plans? Qualifications vary by state, but for the most part, if you receive any kind of government assistance (other than Social Security) or make below a certain amount each year, you can get a free cell phone and 250 free minutes of talk time per month. You'll also receive free voicemail and text messaging! Just visit Assurance Wireless (AssuranceWireless.com) or Safelink Wireless (SafelinkWireless.com) to see if you qualify in your area. *MONTHLY SAVINGS: $100 OR MORE.*

Left your cell phone in a hot car by accident and now it won't work? Just turn on the car's air conditioner and direct it at the phone. When you get home, continue cooling the phone until it is no longer hot to the touch, then put it in an airtight bag and stow it in the fridge (not the freezer) for 5 minutes. Your phone should work again just fine!

Savings amount: $50–$400 for a new phone.

- **Switch your cell phone plan to "pay-as-you-go."** If you find yourself under-using your mobile minutes each month, consider canceling your current plan when your contract ends and try paying as you go instead. With pay-as-you-go phones, you pay an amount of money up front instead of getting a bill each month. Most plans will charge you 5–10 cents per minute and offer discounts if you put a large amount of money (usually $100) on the phone. Pay-as-you-go phones are great for phones that you only use in an emergency and for giving to teens so you can make sure they don't over-text, over-talk, and overspend! Ask at a cell phone or electronics store about these types of phones and promotions. Paying as you go may just fit your specific lifestyle nicely and cut down on escalating cell phone bills at the same time! **MONTHLY SAVINGS: $50 OR MORE.**

- **Change your current cell phone coverage plan.** Having too many or too few minutes on your cell plan can throw your monthly phone statements totally out of whack. Whether you're wasting money by not using the minutes you pay for or racking up insanely high charges due to overages each month, you can try to tailor your cell phone plan with elements that work best for your lifestyle. Check out web-sites such as BillShrink.com, MyRatePlan.com/Wireless or LowerMyBills.com for free cell-phone comparisons aimed at finding a plan that better fits your usage profile. **ANNUAL SAVINGS: $300-$600.**

WHO KNEW?　　QUICK TIP

Need a phone number? Don't dial 411. Text Google the name of the business and it will give you the information! Normal text-messaging rates for your plan apply but you won't be charged any extra!

Savings amount: $1.99 per call.

- **Look online for cell phone purchases.** Conventional wisdom says if you're in the market for a new phone, plan, or upgrade of some sort, then simply get in the car and head to the nearest cell phone store, right? Believe it or not, these stores are the *most expensive* places to buy a cell phone! Because they count on foot traffic and impulse purchases, they're able to price phones much higher than the company's website. Check out your cell phone company's online offerings when it's time to get a new phone and you will almost always find several free or heavily discounted phones that the stores no longer carry. You can also renew and/or upgrade your phone and service plan at Amazon.com (Amazon Wireless) for much less than at the cell store or through your carrier. *SAVINGS AMOUNT: $50–$300.*

- **Refrain from purchasing cell phone insurance.** When purchasing a cell phone, never sign up for insurance or a warranty; subsequently if you're currently paying a monthly fee for insurance, cancel it immediately. The insurance plan of many cellular providers has a deductible of up to $50 that you are responsible for paying, and the phone you'll typically receive as a replacement when yours is out of commission could well be a refurbished model, or an already-outdated model from last year. The cost of taking your chances and buying a cheap replacement (if necessary, or searching ebay sellers for a replacement phone) is usually much less than what your cellular company is offering for you for insurance. *SAVINGS AMOUNT: $5-$60.*

- **Keep your eye on data fee charges.** If your cell phone company charges you data fees, make sure you only do high-data tasks (streaming music and videos, downloading apps, music, podcasts) while connected to a Wi-Fi network. Also, make sure your email account on your phone is set to manually download new messages as your phone constantly checking your email in-box can waste a lot of data minutes! As well as waste battery life.

- **Email your texts.** Did you know that just about every cell phone plan allows you to receive texts by email? Save money on texting charges by emailing a text rather than sending it from your phone.

- **Buy international calling cards.** Your best friend just moved to Italy and you're dreading the toll it's going to take on your monthly phone bill. Before you make that first call overseas, stop! With international calls, never dial directly; instead, buy an international phone card at your local convenience store. Most specialize in a particular country or continent and will allow you to talk for only pennies a minute. You can also go to AITele-phone.com, which works pretty much the same way but also provides the option of prepaying online or receiving a monthly bill. Viva the savings!

- **Stick with the same provider as your friends.** Most cell service providers offer free unlimited in-network calling, which means you won't be charged a dime when you call people who are in your same network. Find out what company most of your friends and family use for their cell phone services and buy a smaller minutes plan with the same provider. You'll save money without sacrificing your gift of gab!

- **Make long distance calls on your computer.** Video chatting over the internet is a great alternative to using the phone. Our favorite service for free video and voice chatting is Skype.com. It's easy to understand, easy to set up, and they offer international rates for voice calls that can't be beat. Google has another great alternative called Google Talk. Check out Google.com/Talk/Start.html for more information.

- **Get rid of your landline.** Although households *without* landlines use an average of 332 more cell phone minutes a month than those with a landline, they still spend an average of $33 *less* per month on basic phone service. Consider going cell-phone-only in your household, especially if you use your mobile as your primary phone anyway. ***ANNUAL SAVINGS: $400–$600.***

TV AND INTERNET SAVERS: STREAMLINE MONTHLY BILLS WITH SIMPLE ADJUSTMENTS

How many of you have signed up for what you thought was an amazing deal on cable and internet, only to get a much-higher-than-expected bill a month later filled with hidden fees and mystery charges? Before you pull the plug on these services, check out the following ideas to help keep TV and internet costs to a reasonable amount.

WHO KNEW?   **QUICK TIP**

Your TV remote just died and you don't have any replacement batteries. Luckily, you can fix this problem with some very fine sandpaper or an emery board that you'd normally use to file your nails! Scrape the ends of each battery until you see some slight scratch marks in the metal. Put them back into your remote and you'll have enough juice to last you the night!

- **Cut back on your channels.** Instead of paying around $150 a month for the top-of-the-line digital cable package, opt for the more basic broadcast channels for $20 or basic cable for $40 per month without premium stations. Most carriers let you add some premium channels for an additional monthly fee. Websites such as BillShrink.com are great places to go to sort out which cable package is best for your household viewing habits. Consider what you want to view and when. You can add that premium channel for the months the show you want to see is on, and then drop it for the months it's airing reruns. As incredible as it might sound to have 900 television channels at your fingertips, our guess is that most of them would go to waste, leaving you with a cable package that grossly outweighs your realistic needs. *MONTHLY SAVINGS: $100.*
- **Share your internet with the neighbors.** Do you and your neighbors both use wireless internet? A great way to save (and share the wealth) is to go in on an internet plan together. If you already have a plan, ask a neighbor you trust if they'd like to pay you for half the cost if you give them the password to your network. You should be able to use the wireless internet hub you currently own, especially if you live in an apartment building. If

your homes are particularly far apart, you may need to extend your network with a second hub or router. *MONTHLY SAVINGS: $20–$30.*

- **Get a Hulu or Netflix account.** Many newer TVs have Wi-Fi. Consider cutting the cable bill altogether and streaming Hulu.com or Netflix.com. You can also visit most network websites and watch your favorite shows online anywhere from minutes to a day or two after it broadcasts.

- **Seek out free wireless on-the-go.** Tons of coffee shops, book stores, hotels, and public buildings offer wireless internet service for free or for free-with-purchase. Find local "hot spots" at Wi-FiFreeSpot.com and don't forget to submit any Wi-Fi zones you find for others on-the-go! This may free you from needing top-notch internet services at home.

- **Bundle all your services into a single plan.** Using one company for all of your home entertainment needs can help reduce your monthly costs by as much as 20 percent. Look into bundling together your landline, TV, internet connection, and cell phone into one plan with a flat monthly rate instead of paying a la carte for all of these services. Most of these flat rates offered by the major service providers tend to be cheaper by hundreds of dollars than paying separately for all of your needs. ***MONTHLY SAVINGS: $1–$60.***

- **Find out the cost of changing plans.** Looking to change your cell phone plan but aren't sure how much you're going to have to pay to get out of your contract? Head over to CellTradeUSA.com which will tell you how much it will cost to cancel. This site also allows you to transfer your contract to another CellTrade user if your cell company allows such transactions.

DAY 11
FINANCIAL FITNESS PLAN
How to Easily Track Your Spending

Today's Financial Fitness Plan is one of the most crucial steps in raising awareness about your expenditures and how to better control them. Tracking your expenses is an incredibly useful tool, especially in cases where the amount you spend can exceed the amount coming in each week or month. Having a better handle on exactly where your money is going doesn't have to be a daunting task. Today we've broken it down into two easy suggestions.

- **Track spending manually.** A good way to start the tracking process would be first to manually organize all of your receipts, expenditures, and incomes so that you know where you stand. File receipts into large envelopes labeled by expense category, then translate these expenditures into a ledger book or spiral-bound notebook under the same categories as on the envelopes. Better yet, enter your spending habits onto a software spreadsheet such as Microsoft Excel and make a point to update it once a week. Establish a routine for maintaining your tracking system—the more you record each expense, the more mindful of your cash flow you will become. Identify which areas are challenging—where you tend to overspend—and make a solid commitment to keeping those categories in check. Maybe you will decide to use cash only for purchases in those problem areas. In any case, once you start at ground zero with a clear idea of what is coming in and what is going out, you can better spend your money in ways that meet your financial priorities.

- **Track spending online.** With multiple expenses coming out of your account on a daily basis in various forms (cash, debit card, checks, credit cards), sometimes an easier way to keep track of everything is with an online application. Services such as Mint.com give you a running snapshot of your spending from all accounts (checking, savings, retirement, investment) at any moment of the day. By connecting to almost any US banking institution in the country, this website gathers all of your financial information into one convenient place and automatically categorizes everything for you, making it a snap to track where your money goes. It breaks down what you're spending, how you're spending, and what is left at the end of each week or month.

Once you begin to track your spending on a weekly or monthly basis using new and/or old-fashioned methods, the way you look at your finances will change. Take control of your expenditures and empower yourself to make smarter budgetary decisions!

DAY 12

MONEY-SAVING SECRETS THEY DON'T WANT YOU TO KNOW

DAILY INSPIRATION

When was the last time a lawyer, an airline, or department store said you were spending too much money? That's why we wrote this chapter. Companies aren't interested in saving you money. We are. And in good and bad economic times, it's often the little tricks that reap the most savings. In this chapter, you will learn all their best-kept secrets.

You have come so far in the last 11 days. Give yourself a pat on the back! Today we get our inspiration from the rich. You may think all billionaires fly private jets to work and eat caviar for breakfast, but many strive to live a frugal lifestyle just like we do. In a TV interview, Ikea founder Ingvar Kamprad said he drove an old Volvo and made a habit of flying coach. Despite being one of Asia's richest men, Indian billionaire Azim Premji stays in company guest houses when traveling; not five-star hotels. Famously thrifty investor Warren Buffett still lives in the same house he bought fifty years ago for about $30,000. These billionaires demonstrate a simple lesson in financial success: Control your spending and keep your fortune. If they can do it, so can you!

SAVINGS SUBJECT
Money-Saving Secrets They Don't Want You Know

TRAVEL SECRETS: YOU'RE GOING PLACES

- **Look on Tuesday for flights**. The Tuesday rumor is TRUE, experts confirm. Deals generally take off for flights and vacation packages between 3 and 4 p.m. on Tuesday. Fire up meta-search engines like Kayak.com and Fly.com to get the quickest overview on the cheapest fares.

- **Focus on reopened hotels**. Hotels that closed to renovate have beds to fill and money to recoup. Far cheaper rates are often available. Don't be shy about contacting smaller places under renovation or recently under renovation and asking up front about possible bargains.

- **Treat the deal as your destiny.** Most of us know that airfares dip in the off-season, but being flexible on your destination can enable you to snag great deals all year. Think of it as planning your itinerary backward. Jump on a good flight bargain to wherever it may go (as long as you approve!) and let all the other economizing on hotel, etc., follow. This is a great way for the adventurous to save big, but sometimes you need to be quick on those flash offers.

WHO KNEW?   QUICK TIP

Playing the waiting game is one great strategy for getting a vacation deal. Choose a destination and register for email alerts, Tweets, and texts from your preferred airline or deal packager for updates on your destination and hotel of choice. When the deal you want to where you want arrives, grab it!

Savings amount: up to 50 percent.

LIFE LESSONS

- **Go to a two-year college first.** Your four-year degree can still bear the name of whatever fancy university where you will eventually graduate. But save tens of thousands of dollars by going to a community college first. You can get some core/required classes out of the way at a far lower tuition while living at home on the cheap.

According to the National Center for Education Statistics, tuition, room and board averaged a total of $13,600 annually at public colleges and $36,300 at private. The average tuition for junior college is $2,963 a year.

- **Cut the ties that put you in a bind.** Everyone knows people who seem to make a sport of asking for money. Being on the Money Diet means making hard choices at the risk of alienating people you care about. Do NOT cosign loans or hand out money to them. "It's not a matter of being an irritation or annoyance. They will harm you—legally and emotionally," Zombie Economics co-author Rick Emerson told DailyFinance.

- **Apply for Aid and Attendance.** Attention, veterans on the Money Diet! An often-ignored military benefit, Aid and Attendance, can supply an extra $2,000 a month for veterans or surviving spouses. Note that A&A is not tied to combat injuries. However, it is designed to provide assistance for daily activities that are becoming too difficult for many reasons. You'll need a lot of documentation and patience—well worth the fight, though. Visit veteranaid.org/elgibility.php for details.

WHO KNEW?　QUICK TIP

There may be a way to get out of that parking ticket you're contesting. Test the old wisdom that says cops don't usually show up for hearings. Ask for several continuances to delay the court date. One attorney insists there's a 30 percent to 50 percent chance the officer won't show when you finally appear. And don't forget to plead NOT guilty.

Savings amount: $10–$50 per ticket.

THIS AND THAT:
THE LITTLE THINGS ADD UP

- **Don't buy bottled water.** Thirsty for savings? Turn on the faucet and turn off an expensive buying habit you don't need. A family of four can spend $400 a year on bottled water, even though it is less regulated and no safer than tap water, according to a DailyFinance report. Need another reason? Despite the cool packaging and marketing, a high percentage of bottled water is tap water. "[People] can save money by not buying as much bottled water and maybe investing in a good filter for their house," say water activist Erin Brockovich (yes, that Erin Brockovich). **SAVINGS AMOUNT: $400.**

- **Get free home-phone forever.** Ooma, a small box into which you plug your Internet cable and phone, enables you to make free phone calls everywhere. It's not a gimmick. Now you'll have a reason to keep your land-line phone! You can get it for less than $190. Visit Ooma.com. *ANNUAL SAVINGS: $450.*

- **Pop new life into pills.** Prescription drugs don't make our budget feel very good. So if we can prolong their shelf life, we'll get more healing bang for our buck. Lots of drugs are still effective five years past their expiration dates. Ask your doctor if any of your meds fall under this category. Also, if a prescription costs less in bigger doses, be sure to get the economy size.

WHO KNEW? QUICK TIP

Schedule regular tuneups for your car. A tuneup can keep an extra 16 to 20¢ a gallon in your pocket, and that number increases with gas prices. Go to fueleconomy.gov for more tips.

Savings amount: $800.

- **Shake, dry, and save.** Give a couple of household items longer life with minimal fuss. Even if your printer's ink cartridge seems empty, shaking it can rustle up weeks of more use. And in the bathroom, frugal warrior Clark Howard recommends blow-drying your razor blades or wiping them down with a towel for extended use. Howard claimed that he used one 17¢ disposable razor for a year simply by keeping moisture away.

- **Lift the burden of fitness equipment.** Pull yourself away from big-ticket items like stationary bikes ($296.32 average cost, according to the National Sporting Goods Association) and elliptical trainers ($586.19). They'll become clothes hangers anyway. And if you already purchased any of the aforementioned, sell it on an online marketplace such as Craigslist.org. Remember: All you need (with a doctor's approval) is 1 hour and 15 minutes of intense activity a week. Or you can take it easier with 2 1/2 hours of moderate exercise.

- **Try rabbit ears on the TV.** Say goodbye to cable and satellite bills. Believe it or not, a pair of old-school rabbit ears can receive many digital channels on HDTVs and other flat screens. You need to be within 35 to 40 miles of a transmitter for indoor-antenna reception, 70 miles outdoors for a roof setup. Enter your zip at AntennaPoint.com to see the nearest transmitters and a program guide. Among ConsumerSearch.com's top antennas were RadioShack Budget TV Antenna ($13), Terk HDTVa ($45) and Antennas Direct DB2 ($35). Just like the old days, you'll have to fiddle with the antenna and its location to get the best reception.

- **Get a DIY divorce.** We're not advocating divorce, but if you and your spouse reach that point, consider a do-it-yourself, uncontested, no-fault divorce. A "pro se" (DIY) is a viable alternative if you don't have kids or big assets. In many states you can access the forms online and submit them for between $200 and $400. It usually takes two to six months for the court to grant the divorce. One prominent attorney told DailyFinance he drew the DIY asset line at $50,000 in the bank and home ownership. Anything more and it might be best for legal eagles swoop in. Note that DIY requires cooperation between you and your spouse—not easy in an emotionally charged time.

KNOW WHEN TO BUY

- **Buy travel insurance at the right time.** There's no hard-set rule on whether to buy travel insurance, but Travelzoo editor Gabe Saglie has a pretty good rule of thumb for the average traveler. Highly anticipated trips like honeymoons that cost $3,500 or more definitely merit coverage. Vacations planned far in advance might also be insured because life has a way of messing up plans over the long term. Travel Guard and Access America are reputable policy carriers but always read the terms carefully.

- **Snag sports deals right before the season.** Cheer up. There's room for big league sporting events on the Money Diet! One all-season plan is to check resell sites like StubHub.com a few weeks before a particular sport begins. Fans who paid for full-season ticket plans get anxious to retrieve a chunk of their investment for tickets they won't use. So they put up blocks of seats priced to move before the opening game. You don't even have to buy them that far in advance! Check in the week prior to the actual game; StubHub often has tickets that members are selling at less than original price.

DAY 12
FINANCIAL FITNESS
Hiring a Financial Planner

Have you ever considered hiring a financial planner? Today we are going to talk about what is involved in hiring one and whether or not you need one. Here are answers to the most common questions about planners:

HOW EXPENSIVE IS A FINANCIAL PLANNER?

Most financial planners charge a flat fee of $120 to $300 an hour for their advice. If they manage your money, they may charge you a percentage of your assets (1–2 percent). Some fee-based planners work on commission, meaning they make money on investments they sell you while also charging a fee. It may be best to avoid this payment system as it puts their salesmanship in conflict with your best interests.

WHAT DO THEY DO?

A good financial advisor will guide you in making tax or investment decisions and help steer you toward your long-term goals. The value of having a professional handling your money is that he/she will bring their experience and objectivity to the table. We don't always see our own money objectively and it can lead to bad decisions.

WHAT QUALIFICATIONS SHOULD I LOOK FOR?

It may be frightening to discover that anyone can call himself a financial planner or adviser. There is no required schooling to achieve this title. Look for someone with more than a securities license which is the minimum designation required to make commission on someone else's investments. Look for someone with a Certified Financial Planner designation (go to CFP.net to use their search feature) or a PFS designation (this is a designation reserved for CPAs who become financial advisers). No matter what designation they have, be sure to confirm their credentials.

WHAT WILL THEY NEED TO KNOW FROM ME?

A good financial planner will want to know more than just your income and assets. They will ask about your investment style (how risky you want to be with your money) and your goals for the future.

If you decide that it's worth the price, finding an expert to help direct your biggest money decision can give you both peace of mind and lucrative returns!

DAY 13
A HEALTHY DOSE OF SAVINGS

DAILY INSPIRATION

Do you feel buried under medical bills? Are you doling out money each month for a gym membership and yoga classes? Do you need new glasses and aren't sure how you're going to afford them? Day 13 is going to give you tons of ways to save on your medical and health expenses, whether you have insurance or not.

Not being able to afford medical costs can be devastating. Feeling like you can't afford to take care of yourself or your family is much worse than feeling like you can't afford nice jewelry or big vacations. Luckily, we're here to help with ways you can lower your costs and even get free health insurance for your children. Remember that life is about how you live it, not about how much money you have. Maintaining healthy habits like exercising and eating healthy can reduce the stress in your life. Feeling helpless about that mound of bills on your kitchen table? We don't believe in retail therapy. Go for a walk or run with the family dog instead and you'll get a natural lift to help you tackle these financial challenges.

SAVINGS SUBJECT
A Healthy Dose of Savings

Because they're impossible to eliminate from your budget entirely, medical expenses both large and small can quickly add up to put you under significant financial stress. Here are some important ways to save on medical and health expenses:

SAVING ON DOCTOR AND HOSPITAL BILLS

If your doctor recommends a medical procedure, you shouldn't put it off because of financial reasons. Instead, look for ways to save on surgeries and hospital stays. Here is a sampling of money-saving tips:

- **Do some research.** Some hospitals are less expensive than others. In general, a not-for-profit facility will be cheaper than a for-profit hospital, so check out the options in your area. Call several hospitals in your area and ask for their billing department to find out the cost of the procedure you need before you schedule it.

- **Don't be afraid to haggle.** It might sound strange to haggle over your healthcare costs, but insurance companies do it all the time, so why shouldn't you? A great resource for finding out how much your medical procedure should cost is HealthcareBlueBook.com. Enter what you are having done and it will tell you how much is reasonable to pay. If your doctor or hospital is charging you more, ask why. If you are uninsured, you should also be aware that most hospitals will be willing to work with you on a payment plan.

- **Consider clinics.** In most cases, an independent health clinic will be your least expensive option for basic check-ups, tests, vaccinations, breaks or sprains, and other non-surgical medical needs. To find one in your area, Google "health clinics" and your town's name, or go to FindAHealthCenter.HRSA.gov to search for clinics via the US Department of Health and Human Services.

- **Take advantage of free help from nurses.** Most insurance plans offer a free "nurse line" that employs registered nurses who can help diagnose your health problem over the phone. Have a fever and aren't sure if it's serious? Not sure if you need to get a tetanus shot after an accident? Call your health insurance company's nurse line for questions like these or anytime you think you may need to see a doctor. If your condition is definitely not dire, they can save you a visit to the ER, and lots of cash. **SAVINGS AMOUNT: $150.**

- **Make sure your kids are covered.** Even if you don't have medical insurance, your children probably qualify for free or low-cost health insurance. Every state in the nation has a health insurance program for children under 18 years old that provides (at little or no cost) insurance to pay for doctors' visits, prescriptions, and much more. To see if you qualify go to InsureKidsNow.gov, then click on "Programs in your state" or call 1-877-KIDS-NOW.

WHO KNEW? 　　　 QUICK TIP

Most follow-up doctor visits are simply intended to monitor your vitals. Save money by asking your doctor if it would be possible for you to obtain blood pressure monitoring, glucose tests, or other needed check-ups for free at your local hospital or even a drugstore.

Savings amount: $100.

CUTTING DOWN ON MEDICAL EXPENSES

Doctor check-ups and medical procedures can have a swift and major impact on your finances, but smaller medical expenses can take their toll as well. Here are some ideas on how to cut down on the smaller costs that will add up over time.

- **Get free medicine.** If you don't have a prescription plan, or if your prescription plan has denied you coverage for an expensive medication, you may be able to get it for free or at a deep discount. NeedyMeds.com will tell you how to get the medicine you need from the government, private outreach programs, and even the pharmaceutical companies themselves. Just find the name of your medication in the "Brand name" or "Generics" list and see if you qualify! When you're prescribed a new medication you should also ask your doctor if he has any free samples on hand.

- **Check for pharmacy discounts.** In order to get customers into their stores, many pharmacies offer discount programs. For instance, Target and Walmart offer $4 prescriptions for 30-day supplies of hundreds of generic medications, while Publix and ShopRite supermarkets offer free diabetes medications and antibiotics. Switching pharmacies when it's time for a refill can also save you money: Many stores offer a free gift card for transferring a prescription.

- **Decrease your copays.** One important thing to know about copays is that they are usually higher if you see a specialist—so it may be worth it to see your GP rather than a podiatrist if you're dealing with a minor issue.

- **Save on prescription lenses and contacts.** The most expensive place to buy glasses is at your optometrist's office. We prefer 39DollarGlasses.com. For around $45 (with shipping), you can get attractive glasses, including the lenses! Walmart also offers good deals on frames and lenses. If you're looking for something more stylish, try WarbyParker.com, which offers good prices on brand name frames. For contacts, check out LensShopper.com. Enter the kind of contacts you're looking for and they'll tell you which discount contact lens site is currently offering the best deal. Order as many boxes as you can at once so you won't have to pay for shipping on separate orders. **SAVINGS AMOUNT: $100–$200 FOR GLASSES, $5–$30 FOR CONTACTS.**

- **Go flex!** Does your employer offer a flexible spending account for health expenses? These accounts allow you to set aside money—that isn't taxed like the rest of your paycheck—to use on health expenses that aren't covered by your insurance. If you don't use the full amount each year, you forfeit it, so it's important to know the wide variety of things you can use these funds on.

WHO KNEW?   QUICK TIP

Did you know that you can use FSA (Flexible Spending Account) money for things like contact cleaning solution, Band-Aids, gym memberships (if you have a doctor's note), humidifiers, heating pads, and even shower bars for safety? Make sure you're using every last dollar of your pre-tax FSA money on these everyday purchases.

Spending amount: 30 percent on every purchase.

SAVING ON DENTAL EXPENSES

In addition to being able to use your flex spending account for dental procedures, there are several other ways you can save.

- **Is your insurance worth it?** With the rising cost of dental insurance, it's time to take a look at how much you're paying versus how much your dentist is charging. If you are doing little more than getting cleanings twice a year and a yearly x-ray, it may be less expensive to simply pay for these services out of pocket rather than paying insurance premiums each month. *ANNUAL SAVINGS: $62.*

- **Get free cleanings for kids.** The first Friday in February each year is Give Kids a Smile Day. Dentists around the country provide free check-ups and cleanings to kids on this day, so if you schedule your kids' 6-month check-ups in February and August, that's one less cleaning you have to pay for! Visit the American Dental Association's website at GiveKidsASmile.ADA.org for more information. *SAVINGS AMOUNT: $55.*

- **See a dentist-in-training.** It's true: you can get that root canal you've been putting off without having to wipe out your savings. Find a dental school in your area to visit for regular cleanings and check-ups, and you'll save big. Be prepared, however, for crowded waiting rooms, long visits, and less privacy. Still, you'll get the care you need at a fraction of the cost. ***SAVINGS AMOUNT: $410 PER CROWN OR FILLING; $35 FOR A CLEANING.***

- **Get a second or third opinion.** It may sound obvious, but few people actually take the time to research whether they truly need the work their dentist suggests. The next time your dentist recommends something costly like a crown, a root canal, or braces for junior, consult another practitioner or two before you start writing checks. Even if your son does need those braces in the end, you may discover that the dentist down the street charges hundreds of dollars less.

WHO KNEW?　　QUICK TIP

If you have a prescription for contacts, you can get a certificate for a free pair of Acuvue disposable lenses at Acuvue. com. Just click on the "Get your free trial lenses" link.

Savings amount: $18–$30.

FRUGAL FITNESS

Here are some of our favorite ways to exercise and stay healthy on a budget.

- **Online dieting programs.** Instead of paying for Weight Watchers, switch to their cheaper online program for about $5 a week. Or try a free dieting site like My-Calorie-Counter.com. Search for the food you're eating by restaurant or type, and enter what kind of exercise you're doing and for how long. Then find out how much you're losing. The site also contains a journal and an online community to help keep you on track. Other weight-loss and exercise sites we like are FatSecret.com and MyHomePersonalTrainer.com. *ANNUAL SAVINGS: $257.*

- **Online exercising.** Instead of paying for classes or buying aerobics, yoga, and other exercise videos, get a free workout online. Check out WorkOutz.com and PhysicalFitNet.com for exercise routines and videos, and DoYogaWithMe.com for free streaming videos of yoga classes. You can also try looking up your favorite type of workout on YouTube. *SAVINGS AMOUNT:$9–$23.*

- **Free ways to exercise.** You don't need a gym membership to get in shape! Find a walking or jogging buddy or just work out at home. Do sit-ups and push-ups before bed every night, do some squats or lunges while watching TV, or turn your stairs into your own personal StairMaster. To make hand weights, take some empty plastic milk jugs and fill them with dry pinto beans. Check out Craigslist.org or Freecycle.org to find people giving away free exercise equipment. **SAVINGS AMOUNT: $50-$150 MONTHLY.**

- **Free yoga.** Yoga is a wonderful way to rejuvenate and relax, but not when it costs a fortune! Luckily, free yoga classes are available each week from Lululemon Athletica stores nationwide. Visit Lululemon.com/community/giftofyoga to find out more about their free weekly classes near you. **SAVINGS AMOUNT: $15-$25 A CLASS.**

- **Stop smoking.** According to the CDC, smokers spend about $15,000 more in lifetime medical expenses than nonsmokers. Imagine what a better, longer, richer life you could have! Find a buddy who wants to quit and resolve to make the change today. There are lots of smoking cessation products (like nicotine gum and patches) out there to help you. Take time to look them up.

- **Go to NatureMade.com.** Nature Made Vitamins has a Wellness Rewards program that allows you to accumulate points when you purchase their products and use the points for vitamin coupons, exercise DVDs, and more. Visit their website at

NatureMade.com and click on "Nature Made wellness rewards."

WHO KNEW? **QUICK TIP**

Many states and cities offer free smoking cessation products (like nicotine gum and patches) or reimbursements to cover their costs. If your state doesn't offer these benefits, check with your employer, school, or health insurance company to see if they'll help you get free or low-cost products.

Monthly savings: $75.

DAY 13
FINANCIAL FITNESS PLAN
When Debt Is Good

In this book we've talked a lot about how to get yourself out of debt, but there are actually times when you *should* go into debt. Today we're going to give you a quick overview of debts that are worth taking on. Good debts include buying things that will increase in value over time, as well as purchases that may extend your income over time. Here's a list of some debts that we consider to be healthy!

- **A home.** A house or condo falls into the category of an asset that will probably gain in value over time, and is one good kind of debt. Of course, you must do all the necessary research to ensure that the house you choose to buy is a good investment and that you can afford it.

- **Education.** Though it's worth considering whether or not a college degree (especially from a non-accredited or for-profit university) can actually improve your job prospects, education expenses are often worth going into debt for. Student loans have some of the lowest interest rates and are some of the best debt to have on your credit report. There are also various tax incentives for accredited higher education to help you get some of your costs back in your taxes. If you think that extra degree will land you a higher-paying job or greater job prospects, then it's probably worth the debt.

- **Health expenses.** Medical bills are one of the most common reasons why Americans are forced to declare bankruptcy. While we hope we've given you some ideas for how to save in this chapter, if your medical situation mandates it, you may have to go into debt. Your health is worth it!

- **Other productive assets.** A "productive asset" is something that can help you or your business gain more earning potential. Some examples may be buying a property you're going to rent out, office supplies for your business, or a computer so you can work on your résumé. If you are buying for your business, remember to keep all your paperwork and receipts. Smaller expenses can help limit your taxable income, and larger productive assets can be depreciated on your tax returns, saving you tax money.

DAY 14

ACCELERATED SAVINGS FOR CAR OWNERS

DAILY INSPIRATION

Take a breath. You're already halfway through your Money Diet journey. By now, you are getting in the rhythm of looking for new ways to save. You already realize that a few dollars here and there can add up to big monthly and annual savings. You are on the right path.

Controlling our finances can be a very scary goal. We often become paralyzed by the "big stuff" like our total debt or the pending cost of our child's college education. Don't let your finances scare you into retreating! You can fix any big problem by addressing many little problems. Think of a necklace that's become snarled. With each tiny knot that you untangle—one at a time— the chain begins to unravel.

WHO KNEW? QUICK TIP

When your keyless remote dies, don't run to the dealer to buy a replacement. Instead, pry open your remote to check what battery it requires. Then head to a hardware or electronics store for a much-cheaper alternative.

Total Savings: $50–$150.

DAILY SAVINGS SUBJECT
Accelerated Savings for Car Owners

Let's begin with one of your most basic needs: daily transportation. You depend on your car for everything. Without it you can't get to work, school, or the grocery store. Here's the problem: Your car leaks money in ways that you probably don't realize. Today it's time to find new ways to stop the leaking.

On Day 14, you will rethink every component of your car usage—from fuel to maintenance to how you drive— and discover cost-cutting strategies in each category. The solutions are surprisingly simple, and will provide you with extra money you never knew you had!

CAR ENERGY SAVERS

- **Lose the excess weight!** Take anything heavy out of your trunk or back seat that doesn't need to be there (kids don't count) and get that extra stuff off your roof rack when you're not using it. An extra 100 pounds in your car can decrease your miles per gallon by 2 percent.

- **Change your air filters.** A clean filter can improve your car's mileage by up to 10 percent. Filters should typically be changed at least every 8,000 miles. However if you live in a sandy or highly polluted area, change it more often. A good rule of thumb is simply to have the filter changed when you get your oil changed.
- **Roll up your windows on the highway.** Having the wind streaming through your hair might be fun, but it increases drag on the car and takes more energy to run. In this case, it's actually cheaper to run the A/C when you're driving over 50 miles per hour.

WHO KNEW?   QUICK TIP

Heated seats in your car may seem like a luxury, but they can actually be a huge money-saver. They don't use as much energy as your car's heating vents to keep you warm. If they aren't offered when you buy your car, consider getting a heated pad for your seat or even having heated seats installed after-market.

SAVE ON GAS

Believe it or not, the way you drive can seriously impact your energy usage. Here are a few ways to conserve gas:

- **Park in the shade.** If you find a shady spot to park on a warm summer's day, you can cut down on the need for air conditioning—one of the most fuel-draining functions of your car. Having to cool your car back down to non-sweltering temperatures uses a lot more gas than you might think! Invest in a sun-blocking windshield shade if you must park in a hot spot.

- **Slow down.** By driving *below* the speed limit, you use less gas. Your car will begin to lose fuel efficiency once it gets over 60 m.p.h. Driving aggressively uses up to 33 percent more gas on the highway and 5 percent on city/residential streets, according to the US Department of Energy. Go a little slower and you'll not only save, you'll be safer.

- **Stop idling.** If you are waiting for longer than 30 seconds in your car, turn off the engine. You use more fuel idling after a 1/2 minute than you use to restart your car.

- **Take the long way.** To save on gas, make one long trip for all your errands rather than several short trips. Not only will you be driving less distance but, according to the Department of

Energy, several short drives beginning from a cold start consumes twice the energy as a single trip of the same distance.

- **Choose your path wisely.** When running errands, pick a route that maximizes fuel efficiency. Avoid any route that has lots of lights, stop signs, or hills. The fewer adjustments you make when you're driving, the less gas you use.
- **Surf the web for cheaper gas options.** Before you fuel up, check out www.GasBuddy.com. Enter your zip code, and this website will tell you the nearby gas stations with the lowest prices. You can also search to find the least expensive pump prices in your entire city or state. They even have cell phone apps! *SAVINGS AMOUNT: 50 cents or more per gallon.*
- **Don't let your tank hit empty.** Try to hit the gas station just as your fuel gauge dips below a quarter of a tank. Having a sufficient amount of gas will ensure your car's fuel injection system stays efficient.
- **Get gas further from the highway.** The gas stations closest to the highway often charge more per gallon than those located a bit off your course—you could save a few bucks by going the extra distance. Don't get hung up on buying from one brand-name gas station, even if you do have

"points" there. The smaller stations typically buy their fuel from the same large oil companies, so the product is of similar quality.

- **Join a fuel rewards program.** If your regular market participates in such a program, you can earn gas savings while loading up on milk and eggs. For example, each time fuelperks! members spend $50 at a participating Winn-Dixie store, a 5¢ per-gallon discount is deposited into their account (For more information, visit www.FuelRewards.com/FuelRewards.html). To join a program online, visit your grocery store's site to see if it participates in a fuel rewards program.

- **Inflate those tires.** It's much harder for your engine to move your car when your tires are even a little flat. In fact, soft tires can reduce gas mileage by 10 percent, according to TireRack.com, a tire sale tracking site. Invest in a gauge and make sure to keep them as inflated as possible without over-inflating.

WHO KNEW? **QUICK TIP**

Only 5 percent of cars actually run better on premium gas. Stick with regular, unless your owner's manual says differently.

Annual savings: $100–$400.

CAR MAINTENANCE

You can take good care of your car inside and out without buying expensive products. Here is how to do it:

- **Shop the dollar store for car care.** These well-marketed items often found in big box home improvement and hardware stores can be unnecessarily pricey. You'll find the same items—squeegees, shams, and sponges—for much less at a dollar store or the cleaning aisle of your local grocery store. *SAVINGS AMOUNT: $5.*

- **Baby oil your leather.** You can eliminate the marks on dashboard plastic by rubbing them with a bit of baby oil. Next, try using that same baby oil on your leather interior. By regularly applying a thin layer, you can prevent the leather from drying out and cracking. *SAVINGS AMOUNT: $5-$10 ON CAR CARE PRODUCTS.*

- **Recarpet for free.** Time to take care of those car mats. Consider going to a carpet store for some samples. You'll always be able to find samples that are gray or another color to match your car's interior and—best of all—they're free! *SAVINGS AMOUNT: $20.*

- **Use a plunger for car dents.** Rub petroleum jelly on the edge of a clean toilet plunger, then place it over the dent and pump it out just like you would a toilet clog. If you can fix a dent this way, you can save yourself a $300 trip to the body shop!

- **Combat corrosion.** When corrosion builds up, your battery struggles to start because of electrical resistance. Luckily, there are several easy ways to avoid such buildup:
  1. **Apply a thick solution of baking soda and water.** Let it stand for 10–15 minutes before washing it off. Baking soda is a mild alkali and will neutralize the weak acid on the terminals.
  2. **Wipe down the battery posts with petroleum jelly.** Try to do this once every couple of months.
  3. **Pour a can of cola over the battery terminals.** Allow it to sit for a half hour, then wipe clean.
- **Add salt!** To ensure that your battery will hold its charge, dissolve an ounce of Epsom salts in 1-1/2 cups warm, distilled water and fill each battery cell. Note: This is only if you have a battery with cell caps that give you access to the battery cell. Some do not.
- **Buy synthetic motor oil.** Synthetic motor oil is cleaner and lubricates moving parts better, meaning it can extend your car's life, especially in cold weather. In many cars, you can even go

longer between oil changes. In fact, most newer model cars can go 5,000 to 7,500 miles without a change. Ask your auto mechanic for more information.

- **Skip your oil change.** According to the American Automobile Association, changing your oil every 3,000 miles (as has often been recommended) is too frequent. Instead, typical drivers really only need to change it every 7,500 miles. *ANNUAL SAVINGS: $90.*

WHO KNEW?   QUICK TIP

Carpools can save you thousands! Use an online carpooling calculator like the one at RideShareOnline.com to see how much you can save. Let's say you commute 50 miles round trip five days per week in a vehicle that gets 22 miles per gallon. You could save almost $5,000!

Annual Savings: $5,000 or more.

CAR REPAIRS

Nothing kills the monthly budget like an unexpected car repair bill. Instead of letting it get you down, start thinking like a repairman so you can fix it yourself or at least be sure you don't get ripped off.

- **Try simple repairs yourself.** Visit AutoMD.com where you will find detailed instructions on simple repairs like adjusting a hood release latch. Be sure you are absolutely certain you understand the instructions before venturing into the garage alone.
- **Know your parts!** Before going to the mechanic's, check out auto parts site NapaOnline.com to bone up on the cost of parts. That will give you a leg up when your mechanic starts talking estimates.

WHO KNEW?　　QUICK TIP

Ignore the pressure number printed on your tire. Instead, follow the directions from the car manufacturer found on the sticker on the driver's side door. Since your car manufacturer knows exactly what number corresponds with the weight of your vehicle, you can get 3 percent better fuel efficiency.

Annual Savings: $81.

DAY 14
FINANCIAL FITNESS PLAN
Identify Your Money Hang-ups

Money and finances are emotional topics for many of us. Our pride is tied up in the amount of money we earn, save, and owe. It can be difficult to deal with our money problems because they stem from how much money we had as kids or how our families dealt with money. Money issues are personal issues. We often equate financial difficulties with "failure" or a lack of responsibility. It's time to change that old pattern and start facing our money hang-ups. We've all got them. The important thing is that we identify and move past them so we can start enjoying a richer life.

Today's financial plan begins with writing a list of your money hang-ups. Start by answering these five questions:

1. Who taught me about financial planning and budgeting?
2. What was the primary lesson I learned?
3. How does this translate into my life today?

4. What money issues do I avoid and why?

5. Do I believe that I can save more money if I try?

Spend some time writing about your feelings concerning money. Look back at anything that is critical and turn it around. For example, if you wrote: "I never like to look at my bank statements because I find them too depressing," turn it into a resolution. Tell yourself that this month you are going to print out last month's bank statement and highlight three areas where you can save. After going through all of your money hang-ups and turning them around, you should feel energized and ready to carry out the next 14 days of your Money Diet.

WHO KNEW?   QUICK TIP

E-Tolls can save you money. You can cut down on fuel costs when you avoid idling in toll lanes. Even better, some toll ways provide discounts as deep as 50 percent to regular commuters.

Savings: 15–50 percent per trip.

DAY 15

BACK-TO-SCHOOL ON A BUDGET

DAILY INSPIRATION

Ready to save on all things school related? Today we look at tips for stopping those school supply spending leaks. Then we alleviate some of your anxiety about the rising cost of college tuition.

By Day 15, you should be feeling in the groove with your new Money Diet. Now it's time to show off a little! You may have already shared some really surprising or interesting savings tips you've learned here with friends or family members. If not, take some time today to do just that. Tell a good friend about one of the money-saving websites we've recommended or post your favorite Quick Tip on Facebook so others can see what an expert you are and they can save big too! Have friends with kids? Read this chapter about school savings and pass the best information on to them. Spreading the word and helping others on their money making quest is good karma. You may find that people reward you by sharing some valuable secrets of their own.

DAILY SAVINGS SUBJECT
Back-to-School on a Budget

From the cost of feeding and clothing them as they grow to the price of sports activities and music lessons, parents can't help but feel overwhelmed by the amount they spend on their children. Don't get us wrong: We love our boys—but we just can't get over how expensive they are! Education is probably the biggest kid-related expense we struggle with. It's also an area of weakness for otherwise thrifty parents: What parent wants to make sacrifices in the area of their kid's education? Thanks to these savings tips, you don't have to. From school supplies to tutoring to college tuition, this chapter will help lessen the burden of educating children of all ages.

SCHOOL SUPPLIES

The average parent forks over about $500 for school supplies every year—and that amount doubles for high schoolers. What if we told you that you don't need to spend that much? Here are some tried-and-true tricks for getting your kid the gear he/she needs without exceeding your spending limit.

- **Buy basic, then personalize!** Stylish and colorful notebooks, binders, and folders cost a lot more than the plain ones, so stock up and then have your child personalize them. They can doodle and draw on them, or add printouts of their favorite band or TV show. For other items like pencils, rulers, and pencil boxes, have your kids apply fun stickers or other embellishments!

WHO KNEW?　　　QUICK TIP

Make your kid happy without overspending on supplies. Buy a plain but sturdy backpack from your local discount or sporting goods store and personalize it with cheap iron-ons from a craft store or Alibaba.com to reflect your kid's personality.

Savings amount: $5–$15.

- **Check your closets and drawers.** Before you go crazy buying everything on your child's school supply list, take 30 minutes to look in all stationary and junk drawers for last year's rubber bands, paper clips, pencils, sharpeners, and so on. Not sure it's worth the time? Uncovering three binders in a desk drawer could instantly save you $9.

- **Stick to the list.** Individual school supplies are fairly cheap, but fill your cart with too many fun "extras" like fluffy pens and bejeweled calculators and you can end up way over budget. It might be best to shop for supplies without your kid. If you do let them come, be ready to say no to expensive luxuries or give them a limit to how much they can spend on special items.

- **Ask your boss.** If your office supply closet is overflowing with excess supplies and you have a good relationship with your boss (this last part is very important), don't hesitate to ask if you can grab some extras for your kids to use.

- **Shop all year.** While there are a ton of sales on school supplies in August, you don't have to wait until August to get the best prices. Check the clearance section of your stationary and office supply store every time you go and stockpile items at greatly reduced prices. This method is better for your budget anyway, since it involves small, regular expenses rather than one giant purchase in August. Remember to store all those discounted supplies together where you can find them in the fall!

- **Wait until after school starts.** If you have a kid who isn't all that concerned about starting the first day of school with brand-new items, skip new purchases altogether or at least allow the first week of school to pass before buying a new lunch bag or backpack. Lots of great items go on clearance just a few days after school starts. Take advantage of it!

WHO KNEW?   QUICK TIP

Skip costly school photos. Find a fledgling photographer instead and help them build their portfolio while scoring free or affordable pictures of your kids. Most will waive their sitting fee and snap away with no obligation to buy. This way, you don't lose any money if the pictures don't meet your standards.

Savings amount: $20–$50.

SPORTS AND ACTIVITIES

Whether it's one activity or several, school activities and organized sports are bound to take their toll on your wallet. Encourage your kids to focus on the extracurriculars that mean the most to them. When they've established their priorities, here are some ways to curb spending:

- **Rent or borrow their gear.** You may be thrilled that Junior is a prodigy on the flute, but instruments are expensive—especially small ones made for growing hands. Rent music instruments from the school, or see if you can borrow from an older sibling or neighbor. Check Craigslist.org as well.

- **Buy used equipment.** New sports equipment is pricey, but you can get good quality equipment cheap when you shop used sporting goods on Craigslist.org. Seek out used sporting goods stores near you and scour local consignment shops for more deals.
- **Keep it casual.** If your child is looking to play basketball with her friends, think about signing her up for a YMCA league rather than a competitive one. She'll get the same playtime, but without the extra competition fees.
- **Limit activities.** It seems like everyone around you is shuttling their kids off to ten different activities, so you feel bad making your kids choose just one. Break free from groupthink and focus on what's good for your child and your budget. Kids should get a chance to participate in the activity they love most, but a schedule packed wall to wall with organized activities isn't healthy for your family or your wallet.
- **Stick to cheaper sports.** This doesn't mean you have to push a particular activity on your kid,

but if his personality is better suited to cheaper pastimes like running or chess club, encourage him to sign up!

- **Buy in bulk.** Talk to other parents about buying gear together. You may be able to negotiate for a better deal with a local merchant or buy in bulk online.
- **Check with the coach first.** Your child's school or team may have a deal with a local sports supply store or company: Ask the coach if you can get a discount ordering equipment through them.

WHO KNEW? **QUICK TIP**

Tutoring doesn't have to be a luxury. Find a friend or former teacher who specializes in your child's area of difficulty. They will charge less and offer the same quality of tutoring as the high-priced centers and services.

COLLEGE EXPENSES: BOOKS, TRAVEL, AND COMPUTER COSTS

Tuition is not the only expense to worry about while your kid is in college. There are living expenses, study aids, computer costs, travel costs, and more. Here are a few trusty ways to save:

BOOKS

- **Skip the yellow books.** Don't pay for those little bright yellow books! You can now read Cliffs Notes free online just by going to CliffsNotes.com. Also check out SparkNotes. com, which has free study guides for hundreds of books as well as free test prep for the SAT, ACT, and more.

- **Visit Chegg.com.** At Chegg.com and other websites like it (they are increasingly popular), you can find huge savings on textbooks. Most also feature a buy-back program, so you can get some money back from each purchase.

- **Get Textbooks Early.** Make sure your college kid has money at the ready the second that college course resource list becomes available. The earlier he/she hits the college bookstore, the more likely it is that used editions will still be available for purchase.

WHO KNEW?   QUICK TIP

Did you know that Amazon.com lets college students rent their textbooks? They also have a buy-back program so that if you do purchase books, you get up to 70 percent back! *Savings amount: up to $500 a semester.*

TRAVEL

If you're going to be shuttling your son or daughter back and forth from college, you may want to consider these savings strategies:

- **Get a travel rewards credit card.** If your son or daughter has chosen a school far from home, you're probably spending lots of money flying back and forth on holidays and school vacation weeks. It's probably time to apply for a travel reward credit card so you can earn points toward your next flight. Look for one that doesn't limit you to a specific airline.

- **Ride share with a friend.** Even if your college student is in driving distance, you may want to suggest a ride-share with other parents whose kid goes to the same (or a nearby) college. You pick them up by car at the beginning of the weekend or holiday and the other family drives them back. This could save you hundreds in gas money every year.

COMPUTERS/LAPTOPS

If you know where and how to buy a desktop or laptop for your college student, you can save hundreds of dollars:

- **Buy laptops refurbished.** If your daughter or son is determined to get a name-brand laptop, resist the temptation to buy new. Refurbished items cost a fraction of the regular price because they are used computers that someone else has bought and returned. Most refurbished computers fall under the same guarantee and return policy as new computers. Overstock.com sells refurbished computers and allows reward members to earn 5 percent in "Club O dollars" on each purchase. Check sites like NewEgg.com and TigerDirect.com as well.

- **Don't buy computers at big electronic stores.** Save yourself a trip to BestBuy. Costco and other wholesale retailers probably sell the same items for less at their stores. Make sure you check online for the best price once you decide on the model you want. Don't be afraid to check Craigslist.org for someone selling a nearly new laptop just because they didn't like the color or because they need some extra money.
- **Skip the extras.** Many people make the mistake of paying for laptop features and power capability that they don't need. Forgo the power upgrade, the Bluetooth capabilities, and the state-of-the-art built-in webcam and put the savings toward tuition.

DAY 15
FINANCIAL FITNESS PLAN
Saving for College

It's difficult to avoid being overwhelmed by the steeply rising cost of college tuition. These days, just one year in academia can cost $10,000–$55,000! And that's just for a bachelor's degree. Don't panic. There are great savings programs out there (like the 529) for those who are planning ahead. There is even free money out there for those with college-ready kids, from grants and scholarships to assistantships. Here are some ways to find it:

WHO KNEW?	QUICK TIP

Believe it or not, there is such a thing as a free college! Of course, they're so rare that they're pretty hard to get into, but it doesn't hurt to try. College of the Ozarks in Missouri, Berea College in Kentucky, and the Cooper Union and the Webb Institute in New York are all 100 percent tuition-free.
Savings amount: $100,000 or more.

LONG-TERM SAVINGS PLANS

If your kids are many years away from becoming under-grads, consider starting a savings with these tips in mind:

- Some states match your 529 contribution. Some even double it! If you want to know whether your state is one of them, go to SavingForCollege.com and click on "529 plans."

- At UPromise.com, you can earn money toward your children's college educations—or help pay off student loan debt already accrued—with your everyday purchases. Register your credit/debit cards along with cards from grocery and drug store reward programs, and then earn points for every purchase you make at thousands of retailers nationwide.

SHORT-TERM SAVING STRATEGIES

These tips are designed for parents of high-school or college-aged children:

- FedMoney.org is probably the most comprehensive online resource on all US government grants and student financial aid programs. Here, you will find detailed information about who can apply for more than 130 government grants and loans related to education. You can also check the US Department of Education's site at StudentAid.ed.gov. To find out all about grants (and how to get them), make sure to visit CollegeScholar-ships.org/grants.

- Check out PrincetonReview.com or Petersons.com. You'll find searchable lists of grants from the lofty (a National Merit scholarship) to the small and silly ($500 for speaking Klingon). **SAVINGS AMOUNT: $500 OR MORE.**

- For local awards and scholarship contests, make sure to check the newspaper and the high school counselor's office for opportunities. This advice even applies to adult students.

- If you know what college you or your child will be attending, ask its financial aid office for an up-to-date list of all merit- and need-based grants and loans it offers. If you think you may qualify, don't be afraid to call up the financial aid department and ask why you weren't offered this grant or loan.

WHO KNEW?   **QUICK TIP**

Many military colleges have not only free tuition, but free room and board. They include the Coast Guard Academy in Connecticut, Air Force Academy in Colorado, Naval Academy in Maryland, and Merchant Marine Academy and West Point in New York.

Savings amount: $100,000 or more.

DAY 16
BIG DEALS ON BIG-TICKET ITEMS

DAILY INSPIRATION

Wow. You are already on Day 16 of your Money Diet. Time to take a moment to celebrate your success!

With a little creativity, you can spend an entire day having fun for *free*. Start by inviting a dear friend or family member to hang out for the day. Treating yourself to time with someone you love is always priceless. Perhaps you could go for a walk at a nearby park, catching up among the birds and trees. Find out if any of the local museums have Free Admission days. Pack a lunch and eat it somewhere unexpected. If you prefer a bit of solitude, swing by the library and pick out a stack of books and videos. Sometimes being a homebody feels more luxurious than the finest spa.

For dinner, jettison the fancy restaurant for a special meal at home. No need to prepare filet mignon or lobster. Instead, make one of your usual dinners but serve it on your fine china (you know, the stuff you never use) and light a few candles. Even Sloppy Joes feel elegant on Lenox dishes!

Whatever you choose, savor the fact that you are rewarding yourself twice: Now *and* when your credit card bills arrive!

DAILY SAVINGS SUBJECT
Big Deals on Big-Ticket Items

High-priced items like furniture, electronics, and appliances allow you even more room to save. With a little bit of knowledge and a willingness to bargain, you can easily avoid spending a fortune on them. To help you, we put together a calendar that works like a cheat sheet, showing you *when* to find the best bargains in each category. We even give you a crash course on how to haggle. Warning: After today, you may have a difficult time paying full price for anything.

FURNITURE

New furniture is a big spending area, but it doesn't have to be. Try these tricks to cut costs:

- **Buy the floor samples.** Ask a sales representative if the store is willing to sell the floor samples (most places do). Often stores have sales specifically for floor samples when the new stock and styles come in, and the salesperson can tell you when that will happen. Otherwise, they may only be willing to sell the floor sample if it's the last piece left. Ask if you can leave your phone number for when the rest run out, and don't be afraid to bargain on the price!

- **Hunt eBay for hidden treasures.** For slightly more unusual items, you'll be amazed at what eBay's antique section can offer. Visit the site for a few minutes each day for a week or two, and follow the bidding on a few pieces you admire. That will give you a feel for where pricing should be when you do start bidding. Don't be afraid to bid on something that needs a little TLC. That's where the real bargains lie!

WHO KNEW?   QUICK TIP

Check out Overstock.com to find hundreds of low-priced furniture items. You'll even get free shipping if you become a "Club O" member or if you buy over $50 in furniture. Plus you can get 5 percent in store credit on every purchase you make.

- **Restore your own antiques!** Find a used treasure at a yard sale or on Craigslist.org, or take that old dining room table in Aunt Sally's attic, and visit HGTV's website at HGTV.com to learn how to refurbish it. Type in a search term such as "refinishing furniture," and you will find many recommended DIY videos. It can be lots of fun!

- **Visit furniture warehouses.** Since the clerks are paid on commission, they may be willing to give you a discount for buying more than one piece. This is a great option if you're looking to furnish a new house or room.

MAJOR APPLIANCES

Know when to get the best deals on appliances and you'll be a better haggler:

- **Demand discounts for accessories.** Most stores have a higher mark-up on the accessories (ice makers in refrigerators or broilers in ovens) for top-selling items so that they can sell the main attraction at a discount. Ask the salesperson if there's any wiggle room; there's a good chance he'll say yes to make the final sale.

- **Shop off season.** Retailers do not have much use for grills in September or space heaters in March. Why not try for a deal on their floor model? Before taking that new Weber home, make sure everything is in working order and none of the parts went missing from the showroom.

Go to EnergyStar.gov and click on "rebate finder." Enter your zip code and you'll be shown all the rebate money you can earn simply by purchasing an energy-efficient appliance or recycling old ones. When we clicked on our zip code, it showed us that we could get $50 just for recycling our old fridge!

Savings amount: $50 or more.

- **Extended warranty not required.** While buying extended warranties for appliances or electronics seems like a prudent decision (and your salesperson will heartily agree), it's rarely worth the expense. Most products do not require repairs during the warranty period and, when they do, the cost of repair is usually about the same as the warranty itself. Why do retailers push for the extended warranty? According to *Consumer Reports*, when stores sell a warranty, they retain 50 percent or more of what they charge. It's more profitable than selling the product itself.
- **If you do get a warranty, read the fine print.** For instance, are you the type who lugs her laptop to every Starbucks in town? You need

a warranty to protect you from theft or that Mocha Latte spilled on your keyboard! *SAVINGS AMOUNT: $73 IN-STORE AND $64 ONLINE.*

ELECTRONICS

- **Embrace nearly-new products!** We go out of our way to buy refurbished electronic ("refurbs"), which are electronics returned, restored to saleable quality by the manufacturers, and then sold once more. Not only do they save cash, but they also provide a similar level of reliability as brand-new items. Whether it's a cell phone, laptop, gaming console, or television, a refurbished item is arguably less likely to be defective than a new one because the factory has already worked out any lingering kinks. Contrary to popular opinion, most refurbished units aren't simply broken items that have been repaired. They may have been returned to the maker for any number of reasons. Maybe it was a returned gift, came in damaged packaging, or was missing a non-essential accessory. If you can live with those things, then refurbished items are definitely for you. Or consider open-box items, a product that the retailer inspected to ensure it was functioning properly and then resold. *SAVINGS AMOUNT: 30 PERCENT LESS THAN NEW ITEMS.*

Haggle for electronics. Before heading to the electronics store, bone up on prices at competing stores or on the internet. If you ask a salesperson to match the price at a nearby store, there's a good chance she will. Make sure you're aware of "extras" that the competing stores may be offering. Even if you're not interested in an extended warranty or free engraving at the other place, you can use the incentive to your advantage when bargaining.

Shop with a spouse or a friend. One person pretends to be really interested in the product, while the other continually points out the flaws and negative aspects. (For many of us, this is how our marriages work anyway!) The "good cop," will keep the salesperson hopeful that he can sell the product, but the "bad cop" will make him work for it.

CALENDAR FOR SAVINGS: WHEN TO BUY

When it comes to finding big-ticket bargains, the question is not "How?" but "When?" Most big-ticket items are seasonal, which means at some point retailers need to unload their perfectly good inventory for the new stuff. Here's when you can pay less for the items you need:

- **January through early February.** Computers and other electronics. Prices drop as companies unveil new products at the International Consumer Electronics Show in Las Vegas.
- **May through June.** TVs, DVD players, portable music players, or other electronic devices. Bargains abound as new products are usually introduced in the late summer and early fall.
- **August.** Outdoor patio furniture and outdoor appliances. Everyone else is stocking up on cold weather gear, leaving plenty of bargains for the patio.
- **October.** Large household appliances and furniture. Businesses are very busy making room for their holiday inventory, and happy to unload last year's merchandise.
- **Black Friday (day after Thanksgiving).** Flat-screen TVs and other electronic holiday gifts. If you are willing to brave the crowds at pre-dawn

hours, Black Friday really does provide the best holiday savings.

- **End of each month.** Furniture. As furniture retailers make their monthly assessment of inventory, they're more than willing to discount any lines they plan to stop carrying.

DAY 16
FINANCIAL FITNESS PLAN
Improving Your Credit Score

A good credit score is key to getting the best financing on a new car or mortgage. If you're a renter, it's also a crucial factor in securing an apartment. Your credit score ranges between 300 (the worst) and 850 (excellent). If you score higher than 650, then you are considered "prime," or credit-worthy, and will be eligible for better loan rates. Day 16 is the perfect time to find out where you stand and, if necessary, clean up that credit rating once and for all. Here are a few simple steps you can take to get on the right track:

- **Get a free credit report.** If you haven't already, get a free credit report by going to AnnualCreditReport.com or calling 1-877-322-8228. Don't be fooled by other "free credit report" sites, which often require you to pay a membership fee. If you want to know your credit score, Bankrate.com's "FICO Score

Estimator" will get you a pretty good free estimate. Otherwise you'll need to pay a fee.

- **Check your report for accuracy.** When looking at your credit report online, you can often click any item directly to dispute it. Make sure all of the addresses listed are current or former addresses, and that all loans and lines of credit listed are yours. If you're unsure, contact the customer service number on the report and ask for more information.

- **Get rid of credit cards you never use anymore.** Do you have credit cards for stores where you rarely shop? Even if you don't carry balances on these cards, having excess credit available can lower your credit rating. Lenders also regard store lines of credit as undesirable because they indicate that you are impulsive. Call the number on the back of the cards and cancel them!

- **Keep your name away from high debt.** If you are listed as a secondary card holder on an account of someone who's racked up a lot of debt, this can negatively impact your credit rating. Unless it's necessary for you to be listed on this account, call the company and get your name taken off.

- **Rebuild your credit.** If your credit report doesn't have a lot of good things to say about you, don't worry. You can change it over time. Make today your day to start: Link one of your utility bills to your credit card. Assuming the bill is pretty consistent (such as water or cable), you will be able to pay this without much worry and you'll be establishing a track record as a prompt payer!

DAY 17

TAKE A VACATION FROM EXCESS SPENDING

DAILY INSPIRATION

On Day 17, we head off for a much-needed vacation. Whether you are driving a short distance or flying half-way around the world, you'll find invaluable ideas in this chapter for keeping your traveling costs down. We start by tackling one of the largest expenses you'll likely have on your trip: airfare. Then we offer our best advice for scoring affordable accommodations, rental cars, cruises, and more. Pack your bags and be ready to save!

Today, as you continue on your Money Diet, remind yourself that your goal is within reach. As Thomas Edison said, "Many of life's failures are people who did not realize how close they were to success when they gave up." It may not look like it right now, but every dollar you save to pay down your debt takes you one step closer to making your dreams into reality. Success is just around the corner, so keep going!

DAILY SAVINGS SUBJECT
Take a Vacation from Excess Spending

TAKE AIM AT THE HIGH COST OF AIR TRAVEL

With charges for checked luggage, carry-on bags, fuel surcharges, on-board meals and drinks, in-flight entertainment, and even "premium" coach seats, air travel these days is more expensive—and more exasperating—than ever. If you learn how to play the game, however, you can start getting a lot more for a lot less.

WHO KNEW? **QUICK TIP**

Pack light and weigh your suitcase before heading to the airport. You may end up with fewer changes of clothes, but you'll save yourself from paying astronomical overweight bag fees. ***Savings amount: $50–$200 per flight.***

- **Be flexible.** Search for trips that begin and end on a Tuesday or Wednesday. We've found that flights throughout the US and Canada are cheaper midweek than on other days.
- **Take a connecting flight.** We know—it's annoying to take a connecting flight when it would be so much easier to book a nonstop one. It can be dull to sit in the terminal for hours on a layover, or stressful to dash from one flight to the next. However, you should consider this option seriously, especially if you can spare the extra travel time. Depending on the destination, it could save you hundreds. *SAVINGS AMOUNT: $100 OR MORE.*
- **Choose a less popular airport.** Look into flying from one smaller, regional airport to another. It's often considerably cheaper than flying into the big-city airports, even if it adds a bit to your driving time.
- **Book on a Monday or Tuesday.** Discounted tickets that were reserved but not purchased over the weekend come back into the airlines' systems on Mondays, and you can snatch up a bargain.
- **Try a travel agent.** It may surprise you, but a travel agent can often get access to lower fares than what you see on the web.

- **Go to Yapta.com.** After you buy a plane ticket, visit Yapta.com. Enter your flight details and they'll email you if the price goes down. Even if you have to pay a fee to change your ticket, fares often fluctuate by hundreds of dollars. This is an easy way to make sure you're getting the cheapest price. **SAVINGS AMOUNT: $50 OR MORE.**
- **Try AirfareWatchdog.com.** If you're looking for the best deals in travel, head over to AirfareWatchdog.com, which catalogs the cheapest fares as they are listed on travel and airline sites. The nice thing about this site is that it polices all the different sites for you, rather than offering fares itself (like Expedia, Orbitz, and other sites). If you normally spend a lot of time trying different combinations of travel dates and nearby airports, this site will take a lot of the guesswork out of it for you.

WHO KNEW?   QUICK TIP

When you're on vacation, save money on souvenirs by staying away from gift shops and stores close to tourist areas. Instead, visit a local grocery store where you'll usually find locally themed postcards, maps, key chains, magnets, T-shirts, and more at regular or discount prices.

HOW TO SAVE ON A HOTEL

The internet is a great resource for checking on hotel prices and amenities. With booking sites such as Expedia.com, Hotels.com, Priceline.com, and many others, you can compare prices and find great deals. In addition, travel review websites like TripAdvisor.com allow you to read customer reviews, so you can look for highly rated, low-cost hotel options you would not otherwise know about. Here are some of our other favorite tips for saving on accommodations:

- **Find the freebies.** Before you book a hotel, look at the amenities it offers its guests, and pick one that gives you the most for your money. For example, you may get a free hot breakfast, free parking, and free Wi-Fi. Here's another surprising trick we've learned: The lower-end to moderate-range hotels are more likely to offer these freebies than a higher-end or luxury hotel, where every service is a la carte. *SAVINGS AMOUNT: $10–$50 PER DAY.*

- **Work the phones.** When digging for discounts on rental cars and hotels, always call the hotel directly for the best deals. If the only phone number you have is a national, toll-free one, look up the local number for that particular location and speak to them directly instead. The closer you get to your travel date, the better. In fact, don't be afraid to call the day before to confirm your reservation and ask for a better rate.

- **Book a room with a kitchenette.** Even if your trip will be short, don't overlook those "extended-stay" hotels. They often have fully equipped kitchens with stoves, refrigerators, and micro-waves. If you prepare one to two meals every day, you could save a lot by eating in. *SAVINGS AMOUNT: $25-$100 PER DAY.*

- **Try a home swap.** Here's a great way to stay some-where new and interesting for free. Do a home swap! You can find many safe, legitimate websites like HomeExchange.com where you can arrange to stay in someone's house while they're staying at yours. You'll have to pay a refundable deposit, but other than that—you're home free! *SAVINGS AMOUNT: $100-$200 (OR MORE) PER DAY.*

WHO KNEW?   QUICK TIP

When searching for travel deals online, make sure to scroll through a few pages of results before making your pick. Many sites have "sponsored results," which means that companies pay to be featured at the top of search results whether or not they match your search requirements.

RAKE IN THE RENTAL CAR SAVINGS

Renting a car this vacation? Follow these suggestions for keeping costs down.

- **Get an online discount.** Looking for online coupon codes for car rental companies? Your first stop should be RentalCarMomma.com. The site collects coupon codes from around the web and helps you find the least expensive options for one-way rentals and rentals in other countries. Another site you can try is RetailMeNot.com/coupons/carrental.

- **Reserve a small car.** If you're renting a car, always reserve an economy car, even though you may need a bigger size. Rental car companies stock very few economy cars, so you'll almost always get a free upgrade. And if you don't, you can just pay the difference at the counter.

- **Don't rent at the airport!** This is our best tip when it comes to saving money on rental cars. Airports charge rental companies concession fees, and guess what? The car rental locations pass them directly on to you. These fees are on top of any tax and insurance you pay and can be around 10 percent more. For a $250 rental, that's $25! You'll save money if you go to an off-airport location in a cab or via public transportation. *SAVINGS AMOUNT: 10 PERCENT OR MORE PER RENTAL.*

WHO KNEW?   QUICK TIP

Find out where the cheapest place to park is at your nearby airport by visiting BestParking.com. This site lets you know about public lots that are close to the airport, but aren't run by the airport itself—and are often half the price.

TRY THESE OTHER GREAT VACATION TIPS

Whether it's a camping trip or a discount cruise, here are ways to have a blast without blowing the budget:

- **Go during the off-season.** The best summer vacation you'll ever take might not be in the summer. As soon as Labor Day passes, the rates go down drastically on hotels and airfare to most vacation destinations. Some of the most-discounted areas are the Caribbean, Hawaii, California, and anywhere else there's a beach. In a warm climate, it will still be as hot as ever on the sand. But the price will be much less, and you'll get the added benefit of having fewer crowds. Check out a travel site like Travelocity. com for good deals to your dream destinations. *SAVINGS AMOUNT: $500 OR MORE.*

- **Save on theme parks.** If you're headed to a large theme park such as Universal Studios and Disney World, your best bet for savings will probably be a package deal. Big attractions almost always offer package deals on, for example, a flight, hotel, and park tickets. These aren't usually significantly cheaper than buying tickets online through a site like Expedia.com or Orbitz.com, but they do often offer added incentives like free transportation or breakfast.
- **Find cheap cruises.** If you're dying to get away on a cruise, check out CruiseDeals.com, which has packages to Alaska, the Bahamas, Hawaii, Mexico, and just about anywhere else you'd want to go on a boat. The company negotiates with some of the world's biggest lines to bring their customers the best rates on cruises. If you want to hit the water, this is the best place to start.
- **Take advantage of student discounts.** If you're aged 12–26, if you're a student of any age, or if you're a teacher or faculty member, you qualify for the International Student ID Card. Available at ISECard.com, the card costs $25, but with it you get discounts on trains, rental cards, tourist attractions, and more. Best of all, they'll provide medical travel insurance up to $2,000.

- **Go camping!** Waking up to the sights, sounds, and smells of the forest can be one of the most peaceful things you'll ever experience—not to mention the most inexpensive vacation you'll take in years. If you've never gone camping, it's time to start! If you don't have any equipment, ask friends if you can borrow theirs. You and your kids will enjoy working together while roughing it (and don't worry, "roughing it" can involve bathrooms and showers, electricity hookups, and even wireless internet). Best of all, with all that hard work each day, plus all the room in the world to run around in, your kids will get exhausted fast! To find campsites across the US and Canada, visit ReserveAmerica.com, and for a great article for first-time campers, go to RoadAndTravel.com/adventuretravel/camping-forfirsttimers.htm.

WHO KNEW? **QUICK TIP**

Instead of an expensive week off, you may get just as much stress relief from a last-minute personal or "sick" day. Convince your friend or spouse to do it too, and enjoy an empty mall, a relaxing afternoon at the beach, or a luxurious brunch (complete with mimosas).

DAY 17
FINANCIAL FITNESS PLAN
Divorce: What to Do

In today's Financial Fitness Plan, we discuss a difficult topic: divorce. Divorce not only wreaks havoc on your emotional and personal life, it can also cause or exacerbate serious financial problems. In the unfortunate event that you are going through a divorce, follow these steps to keep your finances in good shape.

- **Take into account all of your assets, accounts, and debts.** How much money do you have? What do you own? What do you owe? Think about your house, car, investment accounts, credit card bills, savings accounts, and more. Regardless of whether you hire a professional to do it for you, it's good to take inventory so you know whether you're in good standing.

- **Revise your budget.** Now that you're getting divorced, you should take a look at your budget and make appropriate adjustments. If you're used to having two incomes, how will a single income affect what you can afford to spend for housing, food, and other expenses? If you have children, will you be receiving or paying child support? Would your life be more comfortable if you moved to a less expensive home? Will you be taking on any additional debt as a result of the divorce? Consider all of these factors while drawing up a new budget.

- **Monitor changes to your credit.** Get a free copy of your credit report at AnnualCreditReport.com. You can review your reports from the three major credit-reporting agencies to make sure there are no divorce-related inaccuracies. (It does cost money to see the scores but it's worth it.) You and your spouse may share common debts like a mortgage or a car loan. If your spouse got the car and the remaining car payments, you should confirm that this account is removed from your credit report. By monitoring your credit report and reporting inaccuracies, you can help protect your financial future.

- **Ask for help.** Divorce can be incredibly stressful and draining, so don't be afraid to ask for advice and support from loved ones and professionals! They're there to help. Just remember, you're not the first—and you certainly won't be the last—to go through this; you will get through it and get your life back on track.

DAY 18
FIX YOUR HOME WITHOUT BREAKING THE BANK

DAILY INSPIRATION

Day 18 is one of the most important money-savers of the year because it covers the single most valuable expenditure in your life: your home. Every bit of your house needs a certain degree of upkeep to avoid money-gouging renovations—from the floors to the ceiling to the plumbing, and everything in between!

You'll save thousands per year by tackling minor maintenance work and repairs on a regular basis using some of the tips we're about to share.

Today, it's also time to turn your eye to retirement—with no fear! There's a German proverb that says, "Fear makes the wolf bigger than he is." Such is the case with many people and their savings goals. We become so overwhelmed thinking about how far we are from our desired goals that we make the problem bigger than it is. We forget that by taking little steps forward we can slowly make our goals a reality. Thankfully, this book is all about little steps!

DAILY SAVINGS SUBJECT
Fix Your Home Without Breaking the Bank

In this chapter, we'll offer money-saving tips for your tools and appliances—the "small stuff" that can rack up big bills when not working properly. Then we'll learn how to handle plumbing snafus, damaged floors, cracked walls, and faulty doors, all for loads less money than a professional would charge. Last, you'll find fantastic tips for painting your home, another would-be wallet-sucker that's actually very inexpensive when you do it yourself.

TOOLS AND APPLIANCES

The best way to save on tools? Keep them from getting damaged and refrain from buying pricey contraptions that you don't *really* need. Here are some great tips for keeping your tools and appliances in top shape and buying them at a discount.

- **Keep tools rust-free and safe to use.** To remove rust from nuts, bolts, screws, nails, hinges, or any other objects you might have in your toolbox, place them in a container and cover with vinegar. Seal the container, shake it, and let it stand overnight. Dry the objects to prevent corrosion. ***POTENTIAL SAVINGS: ABOUT $250 OR MORE FOR REPLACEMENT TOOLS.***

- **Find wall studs, no tools required!** Looking for a stud and don't have a stud finder? Use an electric razor instead. Most razors will change slightly in tone when going over a stud in the wall. ***SAVINGS AMOUNT: $20-$60.***

- **Use a bottle of olive oil as a leveling tool.** You're hanging a new shelf, but you don't have a level in your toolbox. Luckily, a quick substitute is a bottle of olive oil! Place the bottle on its side and hang the shelf when the liquid looks like it's parallel to the floor. ***SAVINGS AMOUNT: $10-$20***

- **Unstick stuck plugs.** If an electric plug on an appliance fits too snugly and is difficult to pull out, rub its prongs with a soft lead pencil, and it will move in and out more easily.

- **Get appliance info in a snap.** Did your washing machine just break down, and you're not sure if it's still under warranty? Need to replace a part in your dishwasher, but don't know what its specifications are? Want to buy a microwave and not sure what you should be looking for? Appliance411.com is here to help. They have purchasing information (including rebates), FAQs about appliances big and small, and best yet, online manuals and warranty information for just about any model of any appliance. If you're looking for help with any machine in your home, go here first.

WHO KNEW?   QUICK TIP

Plumbing fixtures and other large appliances often come with a lifetime warranty, so do a little investigating before you fork over cash for repairs. Consult the manufacturer first, and there's a chance you'll get a replacement part for free.

PLUMBING KNOW-HOW

Your plumbing fixtures are some of the most expensive items in your home to purchase and repair. From leaky pipes to clogged drains, many plumbing problems can be solved without seeking professional assistance. Here are some easy tips to keep your pipes in good working shape—without sending your savings down the drain!

- **De-clog sinks with dish soap.** If your kitchen sink is clogged and you think grease might be the culprit, flush it out with the biggest grease-fighter in your home: dishwashing liquid. Squirt a generous amount down the drain, then immediately pour a pot or kettle full of boiling water after it. Repeat as necessary until the clog is gone!

- **Ditch the Drano.** Most people know the old science fair project of mixing vinegar and baking soda to cause a chemical reaction worthy of a model volcano, but not many know that this powerful combination is also a great drain cleaner. Baking soda and vinegar break down fatty acids from grease, food, and soap buildup into simpler substances that can be more easily flushed down the drain. Here's how to do it: Pour 2 ounces baking soda and 5 ounces vinegar into your drain. Cover with a towel or dishrag while the solution fizzes. Wait 5–10 minutes, then flush the drain with very hot water. Repeat until your drain is clear. *SAVINGS AMOUNT: $10–$15 FOR DRAIN CLEANING SOLUTION.*

- **Maintain a healthy drain.** Don't wait until your drain gets clogged before you flush out grime, grease, and hair. Perform monthly maintenance with the help of a little yeast. Pour two packets of dry yeast and a pinch of salt down the drain, then follow with very hot water. Wait half an hour, then flush again with hot water. The yeast reproduces and expands, which breaks up stubborn grime and hair clogs and saves you from calling the plumber. **SAVINGS AMOUNT: $150.**

- **Quiet down those noisy pipes!** If your water pipes are banging and pounding, you may be able to get rid of the noise without paying for a plumber to visit. First, turn off your main water valve, which is usually located near the water meter. Turn on all your water faucets, set them to cold, and let them drain until dry. Then close them again. Turn your main valve back on, then turn each faucet back on as well. After making spitting and coughing noises for a few moments, they should now flow freely with no noise coming from the pipes. **SAVINGS AMOUNT: $150.**

- **Fix pipe leaks without the costly supplies.** Instead of using expensive Teflon tape to prevent leaking between pipes and other parts that screw together, just use dental floss. Wrap the floss around the item's threads, and you'll have a tight connection. **SAVINGS AMOUNT: $5 PER ROLL OF TEFLON TAPE.**

If one of your roof's shingles has fallen off, you can make a temporary replacement using duct tape. Cut a 1/4 inch-thick piece of plywood to match the same size as the missing shingle. Then wrap it in duct tape (you will need several strips), and wedge it in place. Use extra duct tape to keep it there, if necessary.

Savings amount: $25–$35 for one bundle of shingles.

FLOOR FIXER-UPPERS

Over the years, your floors will take a greater beating (literally) than anything else in your home. Unluckily for us, floors are incredibly expensive to replace and refinish. Fortunately, you can ward off big spending on floor repair by undertaking the small repairs and basic upkeep yourself—they're fairly simple to handle and the savings will be big! The more care you put into your floors, the more you'll get out of them. Here are some great, easy fixes for floor troubles that'll help preserve your hardwood and tiles as long as possible.

- **Iron away dents in wood floors.** As long as the wood hasn't broken apart underneath, you may be able to fix dents in wooden floors or furniture.

Here's how: Run a rag under warm water and wring it out, then place it on top of the dent. Apply an iron set on medium heat to the rag until the rag dries out. Repeat this process until your dent is gone.

- **Silence a squeaky floor.** If that squeak in your floor is about to drive you crazy, it may be time to repair it yourself. Most squeaks are caused not by the floorboards themselves, but by the support beams that hold up your floor, called joists. To fix a squeak, first find the joist closest to it using a stud finder or a nail. Joists are usually located 16 inches apart and run lengthwise from the front to the back of your house. Once you find the joist, drill a number 8 wood screw through the floor into it. This should fix your problem. *SAVINGS AMOUNT: $20-$300 IN FLOOR REPAIRS.*

- **Fill a hole in your vinyl floor.** If there's a small hole in your vinyl floor, here's how to patch it up without anyone noticing the spot: Find a tile that is the same color, or better yet, one that you've saved for a replacement. Make some vinyl shavings from the tile using a cheese grater, then mix them with a small amount of clear nail polish. Dab the nail polish mixture into the hole and let dry. Voilà! Your floor is like new again.

- **Restore vinyl flooring with a hot iron.** If your vinyl flooring is coming up, put it back where it belongs! Lay a sheet of foil on top (shiny side down), then run a hot iron over it several times until you feel the glue on the bottom of the tile starting to melt again. Place something heavy, like a stack of books, on top and leave it overnight to set. *SAVINGS AMOUNT: MORE THAN $1,000 FOR 200 SQUARE FEET OF NEW FLOORING.*

WHO KNEW?   QUICK TIP

Rein in remodeling costs! If you're planning a big remodel of your home but don't want to spend a bundle, try to keep major plumbing appliances like toilets and kitchen sinks where they are. These types of improvements can cost around $1,000 apiece and could be a major portion of your renovation budget.

Savings amount: $1,000 or more
for each plumbing fixture.

WALLS AND DOORS

See some cracks in your walls or ceilings? Squeaky or sticky doors? No problem. While you *could* spend hundreds on a carpenter, these small signs of damage can be repaired on your own with little trouble and only a few inexpensive tools. Check out our simple money-saving tips for repairing walls, ceilings, and doors.

- **Patch up walls with homemade putty.** To make a putty for quick patches, combine a tablespoon of salt with a tablespoon of cornstarch. Mix them together with just enough water to make a paste. Apply while still wet.

- **Cover cracks with faux plaster.** If you spot a crack in your ceiling, but you can't quite afford to re-plaster yet, you can fake it with some readily available household supplies. Take one part white glue and one part baking soda, mix them together thoroughly, and then dab the paste onto the crack using your fingers, a Q-tip, or similar object. If your ceiling isn't white, you can try mixing different food colorings into the paste until you get exactly the right shade. ***POTENTIAL SAVINGS: $300 OR MORE FOR PROFESSIONAL RE-PLASTERING (PER AREA).***

- **Say "no more" to sticking doors!** Your bedroom door has expanded, and realigning the hinges didn't work. Instead of taking the entire door down to sand the bottom, try this trick instead. Place enough newspaper under the door until it can just barely close on top of it. Then tape a piece of coarse sandpaper on top of the newspaper, and open and close the door until it glides over the floor without a noise.

- **Grease up squeaky doors for free.** If your doors shriek every time you open them, don't run to the store for WD-40. Squeaky doors can be silenced with a little hair conditioner wiped on the offending hinge. Now your entryways will be as tame as your mane. *SAVINGS AMOUNT: $8.*

WHO KNEW?   QUICK TIP

Prevent extra paint in the can from drying up with this crafty maneuver: Blow up a balloon until it's about the size of the remaining space in the can. Then put it inside the can and close the lid. This will reduce the amount of air in the can, thus prolonging the paint's freshness.

Savings amount: $20–$40 per gallon of paint.

PAINTING THE HOUSE

You don't need to hire a pro to get a great paint job. Painting your own house is one of the easiest ways to save cash on home maintenance projects—and it can be fun too! Here are our favorite money-saving tips for your next painting venture.

- **Test-run paint colors on your computer.** If you subscribe to Behr's free "Paint Your Place" app (Behr.com), you can give any room in your house a virtual paint job—simply upload a photo of the room and start virtual painting. Experiment with colors until you find the perfect scheme for your room, then save the photo, along with your paint choices, for future reference.
- **Keep paintbrushes in tip-top shape.** Old, crusty paintbrushes put a cramp in our paint projects. To soften those bristles, we soak them in full-strength white vinegar and then clean them with a comb. To prevent brushes from hardening in the first place, rub a few drops of vegetable oil into the bristles after using and cleaning. *SAVINGS AMOUNT: $5-$20 FOR REPLACEMENT PAINTBRUSHES.*
- **Strain your paint to avoid lumps.** Use the lid of the paint can as a stencil to cut a circle out of a screen that will fit perfectly inside the container. Push down with a stir stick as far as it will go so the lumps will be out of the way at the bottom.
- **Line paint pans with foil.** There's no need to spend your money on disposable paint liners for your roller pan. It's just as easy to line the pan with aluminum foil—and a lot cheaper, too. *SAVINGS AMOUNT: $2-$10.*

If your DVD player is holding a DVD hostage and won't spit it out, you may be able to fix it yourself without heading to the repair shop. Look next to the DVD tray for a tiny hole, then stick the end of an unfolded paperclip into it. It should activate the player's emergency tray opener, allowing you to stick another DVD in there and try again.

DAY 18
FINANCIAL FITNESS PLAN
Set Your Savings Goal
for Retirement

Your lifestyle in retirement depends on the financial decisions you make now. But how do you know
what amount/goal to save each year so you'll be able
to live comfortably post-career? It's a projection
into the (sometimes) distant future, and it can be a
nerve-wracking one to make. You need to account for
all the years you expect to live past retirement (20?
30? 40?), your desired standard of living, the rate of
inflation when you retire, future medical costs, and the
hoped-for returns on your investments. If this sounds
complicated, you're right. It is.

Some financial pros say that you'll need 70 to 80
percent of your final income per year in order to sus-
tain your pre-retirement lifestyle. Keep in mind that
your expenses will change as you get older. Your kids
will be adults with families and homes of their own and
you may finally pay off the mortgage. On the flipside,

you'll have to prepare for increasing medical bills and all those carefree activities you've fantasized about for your entire adult life: travel, second homes, etc. Take all of these lifestyle changes into account and remember to consider inflation—increasing rates can be hard to estimate in advance, but they will certainly affect the value of your savings.

Overwhelmed? Don't be. There are some great tools at your disposal to help you determine the numbers:

- **E*Trade's retirement planning calculator.** https://us.etrade.com/e/t/plan/retirement/quickplan
- **AARP retirement calculator.** http://www.aarp.org/work/retirement-planning/retirement_calculator/
- **Kiplinger's retirement savings calculator.** http://www.kiplinger.com/tools/retirement-savings-calculator.html

No matter what figure you set as your goal, we hope your Money Diet helps you to save towards it starting now and that you begin to feel more and more confident about the future.

DAY 19
PARTY MORE, SPEND LESS

DAILY INSPIRATION

"Worry, like a rocking chair, will give you something to do, but it won't get you anywhere." —Vance Havner

On Day 19, we are going to talk about how to save money on all kinds of parties and celebrations. But first we need to internalize the wisdom in the quote above and put aside our worries and all the money stress that keeps us rooted in place so that we can start fresh. Consider all the moments in your life that you have spent worrying about paying bills, saving for college, getting out of debt, and making those rent payments or mortgage payments when times were tough. Imagine if you could get those moments of your life back and replace them with a brighter, more positive and productive mindset. Imagine if you had instead stayed up and made a list of hundreds of ways to make your situation better. Today is different because you have that list right in front of you. No more rocking in place. Today you're going to make progress.

DAILY SAVINGS SUBJECT
Party More, Spend Less

GROWN-UP PARTIES DONE RIGHT

A party is about the people, not how much you spend on it. Before you throw a huge bash, write out your priorities in terms of what you think is most important to spend your money on (for example, the least on decorations and the most on food). Then figure out how much you're willing to spend on the highest item on your list, and work your way down. Friends will always ask, "Can I bring anything?" Take your good friends up on the offer and have them bring a dessert or appetizer. And don't forget—potlucks and picnics are cheap and always popular. Here are more tips to help you save:

- **Find party entertainment at a college.** If you're hosting a party that requires you to hire someone like a clown, face painter, or bartender, head to your local college first. There, you'll find hundreds of young people who will do the job for a lot less than a pro. Put up an ad near the cafeteria and stop by the careers office to see if they have an online "bulletin board." **SAVINGS AMOUNT: $50.**

- **Don't buy too much food.** Wondering how much food to make for your big soiree? Wonder no longer. At a cocktail party (no dinner served), 10–12 bite-sized portions per person is a good bet. If you're also serving a meal, figure on 4–5 bites per guest. For dip, figure 2 tablespoons per person (plus veggies or crackers for dipping), and for cheese, get 4 ounces for each person. **SAVINGS AMOUNT: $10 OR MORE ON WASTED FOOD.**

WHO KNEW?   **QUICK TIP**

PaperlessPost.com can save you money on invitations and impress your friends. Go to their website to design your free invitation and email it to all your guests. The best part: When your guests click on the virtual invite, it opens like a real card!

Savings amount: $20 or more.

- **Save on ice.** If you run out of ice at a party, you're in trouble! But how do you know how much to buy? Use this simple metric. If you're serving mostly cocktails, the average person at a party will go through 10–15 cubes. When you buy ice cubes in a bag, you will get about 10 cubes per pound. **SAVINGS AMOUNT: $4 IN EXTRA ICE.**

- **Stick with appetizers.** Who can afford catering costs or serving dinner to dozens of guests? Appetizers are preferred by guests anyway because they allow for easy nibbling. Buy frozen appetizers in bulk at the nearest Costco or grocery store and save a ton.

- **Opt for a brunch party.** Get out the big griddle and start flipping some pancakes. Cook a big quiche for everyone to enjoy. You'll inevitably spend less hosting a morning event with cheaper food options like these.

- **Don't waste the punch!** Drinking punch that's half water is never fun, but ice cubes can melt so quickly when left out in a bowl. One of the easiest ways to keep a large punch bowl cold is to make larger ice cubes, as it will take one giant ice cube much longer to melt than many little ones. To make a long-lasting, large cube, fill a rinsed-out milk or juice carton half-full with water. Then peel off the cardboard when it's time to use.

- **Save every drop of wine.** Here's a neat trick to save the little bit of wine at the end of the bottle. Freeze leftover wine in ice cube trays, then store the cubes in a freezer bag. Use them in wine coolers and any dish that calls for wine. **SAVINGS AMOUNT: $4 ON COOKING WINE.**

Wondering how to get the most out of your leftover wine (besides drinking it, of course)? Keep it fresh by putting whatever is left in a small container such as a jam jar. This limits the amount of air the wine is put in contact with, keeping it fresh. Incidentally, that is the same thing those expensive "wine vacuum sealers" do!

Savings amount: $19 on vacuum sealer.

- **Keep the BBQ lit longer.** When the coals start to die down on your grill, don't squirt them with more lighter fluid, which not only costs money but can leave your food tasting bad (not to mention burn the hair off your arm). Instead, blow a hair dryer on the base of the coals. The hair dryer acts as a pair of bellows, and your fire will be going again in no time.
- **Makeshift platter.** If you're looking for a platter for deviled eggs, brownies, or other picnic items, simply cover a piece of corrugated cardboard with aluminum foil (dull side up), then throw it

away when you're finished! ***SAVINGS AMOUNT: $3 ON A PLASTIC PARTY PLATTER.***

- **Perk up your tabletops.** Linoleum or vinyl floor tiles are excellent for covering picnic tabletops. You can also use linoleum on kitchen shelves instead of contact paper. It will last longer and is easier to keep clean.

- **Stick to a theme drink.** Alcohol can be costly when you're trying to suit everyone's individual tastes—especially when you don't know who will drink what. Let them drink according to a chosen party theme and you'll save yourself a lot of guesswork as to how much alcohol you need. You'll also be allowed to take advantage of the discounts you get from buying in bulk.

CAKE WISDOM

Store-bought or homemade? That's usually the question when it comes to party planning. Most of us know that the cost-saving answer is almost always homemade. What you don't know is that there are some great tricks for making a cake live up to the best bakery standards.

- **Ice like the pros.** Making a birthday cake at home is a great way to save at the bakery, but if you're not a cake-decorating genius, it never looks as good as store-bought! To give the icing on top of your cake the silky look of a professionally made one, ice it as usual and then blow a hair dryer over the top for a minute. It will melt the icing slightly, giving it the shiny appearance you're looking for. **SAVINGS AMOUNT: $26.**

- **Decorate cakes like a pro.** Here's a great bakers' trick to make it easier to decorate the top of a cake: With a toothpick, trace the pattern, picture, or lettering before you pipe the icing. This guide will help you make fewer mistakes.

WHO KNEW?　　　QUICK TIP

Save on kids' party favors by including an inexpensive craft at the event. Popsicle stick photo frames will keep their energy focused during the party and make a great take-home prize.

Savings amount: $10–$20.

- **Rescue a layer cake.** You decided to attempt a three-layer cake, and can't believe how great it looks. The problem? The layers are sliding so much it's starting to look like a Jenga game waiting to topple. Don't give up and waste $26 on a store-bought cake. Fix by cutting two straws so they're just shorter than the height of the cake, then inserting them and frosting right over them (use four strays if it's really shaky). If anyone notices your cheat, they'll just be impressed!

- **Prolong the life of a cake**. If you need to make your cake a day or two before the party, put half an apple in the container. It will provide just enough moisture to keep the cake from drying out before everyone enjoys it.

WHO KNEW? QUICK TIP

Share a birthday party rental with a friend. Bouncy house rentals have become popular at kids' parties, but renting them is expensive. Find a friend whose child has a birthday that same month and share the cost. One can host the bouncy house party and the other can provide the food!
Savings amount: $100 or more.

KIDS' BIRTHDAY PARTIES

The average kid's birthday party can cost upwards of $250. Make some new budget-friendly choices the next time you host one:

- **Choose cupcakes.** Consider serving cupcakes instead of one large cake, which will eliminate the need for forks and paper plates—and save you money. *SAVINGS AMOUNT: $5-$10.*

- **Party on a weekday.** If your children's birthday parties are putting a hurt on your budget, there's a simple solution—have the party during the week instead of on a weekend. Your child will have just as much fun as they would at a weekend party, maybe even more, since it's a rare weekday treat. *SAVINGS AMOUNT: $25 OR MORE.*
- **Host at a ballpark.** A great, but rarely utilized, location for a summer party is your local minor league baseball park. Tickets are cheap, kids will love interacting with the mascot, and there's no need to stay the whole game—five innings or so should suffice. The team might even offer you discounted group tickets and flash your child's name on the scoreboard.

WHO KNEW? **QUICK TIP**

Many party stores now sell helium tank kits for about $35. One tank provides enough helium for 30 nine-inch latex balloons (included). Buy that many balloons at a florist and you're bound to pay $50 to $60.

Savings amount: $15–$25.

DAY 19
FINANCIAL FITNESS PLAN
Find Technology to Help You

There are a ton of computer applications out there to help you manage your Money Diet. You may not be ready for all of them, but today is a good day to experiment with at least one. Here is a list of online tools that can support the changes you want to make this month.

- **Mint.com** can pull from all your online accounts to show your personal spending trends in just about every category. Want to see how much you spent on clothes last month as compared to this month? Mint.com will present you with all kinds of colorful graphs that represent your money choices and help you budget. You have to give this website your account passwords in order for it to do its trick, but doing so will prevent you from having to enter lots of information. When you download this application to your cell phone, you can check all your accounts at a glance whenever you feel like it. Want to know your current net worth? It can do that too! It uses Zillow.com data to access your up-to-date property value.

- **Quicken.com** is another popular tool for managing personal finances. You don't have to give this service your passwords, but it does need you to input information about your accounts.

- **ReadyForZero.com** does a great job motivating people to pay off debt. It sends you messages alerting you on your progress as you pay down a specific debt and posts a golden trophy as a pat on the back when you finally pay it off!

- **SmartyPig.com** is an interesting website that offers encouragement and rewards as you save for a specific goal. It's free (like all the above services) and it's extremely helpful whether you're saving for a wedding, a vacation or a flat-screen TV. When you succeed in reaching your goal, it even rewards you with extra spending points that you can transfer to your bank account or get back as gift cards.

- **PearBudget.com** is a very straightforward site for creating a budget for those who are easily overwhelmed. It's a great place to track how you're spending on the Money Diet.

DAY 20
SAVINGS SECRETS FOR PET OWNERS

DAILY INSPIRATION

"Too many people spend money they haven't earned, to buy things they don't want, to impress people they don't like." —Will Smith

We live in a consumer culture where how much you spend defines how others perceive you. Do you find yourself over-extending your bank account with big-ticket purchases just to feel like you're keeping up with the Joneses? Do you consistently stock your closet full of expensive, name-brand clothes when in reality you're most comfortable wearing a T-shirt and jeans from the department store down the street? These are prime examples of overspending, overdoing, and overindulging to impress others and most of us are guilty of them and others like them. The Money Diet requires that we have enough courage to go against the grain. Your decision to make better choices this month may not be popular with everyone but keep in mind that spending tons of money on things to impress others adds unnecessary stress to your life and puts you further in debt. In order to let go of this way of thinking and streamline your expenditures, keep your eye on the prize. Think about that giant pile of money you'll have saved after you've employed some of these simple tips.

DAILY SAVINGS SUBJECT
Savings Secrets for Pet Owners

For 2012, it is estimated that a total of $52.87 billion will be spent on America's pets! According to the US Census Bureau, the average family spends $58 per month keeping our animal friends fed and healthy. While we clearly adore our furry family members, there are tons of cost-saving ways to ensure their well-being without paying through the nose.

WHO KNEW?   QUICK TIP

Walking your dog at night doesn't mean you need to invest in a fancy nighttime collar. Simply cover a regular collar with reflector tape and watch Rover glow!

Savings amount: $5–$10.

MEDICAL COSTS

We all love our pets and will go to any lengths to make sure they are happy and healthy, but this shouldn't mean taking on credit card debt to pay vet bills. Here are some effective ways to bring veterinary costs down:

- **Find low-cost vaccination clinics.** Is your pet in need of vaccinations that you can't afford? Low-cost vaccination clinics are a wonderful way to save money on vaccinating your pet because they cost much less than your friendly neighborhood vet. Check out LuvMyPet.com to find a directory of reduced-price veterinary clinics around the US or check with your local animal shelter to see what vaccination services they provide. If you're committed to using a vet, keep in mind that some local veterinarian's offices may offer discounted vaccination days. ***ANNUAL SAVINGS: 25–60 PERCENT OFF VACCINATION COST.***

- **Use veterinary schools.** Routine vet visits can run anywhere from $50–$90 just to have your pet seen, never mind additional work that may be required. Save on regular check-ups by taking your pet to a veterinary school instead. These vets-in-training are supervised by licensed veterinarians, so you can get good care for much less. Call a vet school in your area to see if they offer clinics for the community. You can find one near you on the American Veterinary Medical Association's website (Avma.org) or at VeterinarySchools.com.

- **Seek out discounted medications online.** Pet medications are often incredibly expensive. Luckily, we've discovered Omaha Vaccine, which offers great deals on meds that cost more elsewhere. Visit OmahaVaccine.com to search for your pets' medications and get free shipping for orders over $35. *SAVINGS AMOUNT: 25–50 PERCENT.*

WHO KNEW?　　QUICK TIP

If your cat or dog has horrible breath, try adding some fresh chopped parsley to his food as a much cheaper alternative to the expensive food additives you find in pet stores. *Savings amount: $20–$40.*

FRUGAL WITH FOOD

The American Pet Products Association estimates that we will spend $20.46 billion on pet food in 2012. Trim these statistics with the below saving tips:

- **Buy pet food at your local grocery store.** When shopping for pet food, make sure to compare prices at the pet store to those at your grocery store or bulk warehouse store such as Sam's Club or Costco. A recent study found that pet food tends to cost more at stores that are full of people who are already buying pet products!

- **Use dog or cat food as treats.** Dogs don't care if their treats are in the shape of a bone. They just want a yummy reward. The truth is, doggie treats have almost the exact same ingredients as dog food, and most dogs can't tell the difference. Instead of paying extra for dog treats, keep a separate container of dog food where you normally keep the treats, then give your dog small handfuls when he's done something reward-worthy! Also, most fresh fruits and veggies are healthy treat alternatives that are generally well liked by dogs and some cats. You should always check with your vet first to make sure your people-food plan is safe for your particular pet and ask them to help you identify the best options. Lastly, ice cubes make good treats for their high entertainment value—and they're free! Change it up by freezing chicken or beef broth into cubes for an extra special reward. *SAVINGS AMOUNT: $5 FOR A BOX OF TREATS.*

- **Make your own pet food.** If you are using commercial wet foods to feed your pet, then it may cost you about $5 a day for a medium-sized dog. Homemade pet food costs about half that price, so it's worth the change. Not only are the savings considerable, but the ingredients used are simple and healthy! Check out online websites such as Allrecipes.com for pet food recipes that cost just $2 a day and give your animal friends something new! *MONTHLY SAVINGS: $90.*

WHO KNEW?   QUICK TIP

Entice dogs to eat any food with beef jerky. If you've bought a new brand of food and your dog doesn't want to eat it, put a piece of beef jerky in the bag and reseal. By the next day, the smell will have worn off on the food, making it seem much more appetizing. This saves you money on a new bag of food and gives your dog jerky-infused dinner. Win-win!

Savings amount: $20 for a bag of food.

FLEA FIXES

Where there is an itchy pet, there are usually fleas. Flea bites left untreated can lead to irritated raw skin and, in some cases, infection. What does that translate to? Vet visits, antibiotics, and lots of cash flying out of your wallet. Stop fleas from raiding your dog and draining your wallet using these suggestions:

- **Add vinegar to their water bowl!** Does your pet have a history of frequent flea issues? Adding a teaspoon of apple cider vinegar to his water each day may help. The vinegar will make your pet's skin more acidic and therefore less hospitable to fleas. As always, you should check with your vet first before changing your pet's diet! *SAVINGS AMOUNT: $12–$100 FOR FLEA COLLAR AND MEDICATIONS.*

- **Make your own flea bath.** You can remove pesky fleas from your pet's coat without having to pay for expensive flea collars or medications. Simply bathe your pet in salt water and the fleas will stay away. You can also try steeping rosemary in warm water and using that as bathwater. Better yet, use a combination of the two! *SAVINGS AMOUNT: $12–$100 FOR FLEA COLLAR AND MEDICATIONS.*

- **Use your vacuum to rid the house of fleas.** You've found a couple of fleas on your beloved pet and suddenly feel like your house is under siege. Before you pick up the phone to call an exterminator, try looking no further than your hall closet. Fleas can be eliminated very effectively from upholstery and carpets by vacuuming with a high-powered vacuum cleaner containing a bag that seals well. Remove the bag and dispose of it outside as soon as you finish or, if using a canister, empty outside and put it back. Also washing pet bedding in hot soapy water once a week is another helpful step to take before spraying your house with the best flea spray money can buy. Savings amount: **$10-$200 FOR FLEA SPRAY AND/OR EXTERMINATOR.**

WHO KNEW?   QUICK TIP

Cats love toys and they aren't picky about where they come from or how much they cost! Instead of spending oodles of cash on feline entertainment, stick a balled up piece of paper, a cork, a jingle bell, or a favorite old toy inside a Kleenex box or a paper bag. Cats will love sticking their paws inside to try to fish out the toy!

Savings amount: $5.

SHAVE COSTS ON GROOMING

Regular professional grooming is an important way to prevent your pet from developing medical problems from things like matted hair and overgrown nails. Forking over $25–$50 a month in grooming costs isn't good spending, so here are some ways to trim those figures:

- **Visit the groomer midweek for discounted services.** The busiest days at the pet groomers are Friday, Saturday, Sunday, and Monday. Find a groomer who offers discounts on Tuesdays–Thursdays or ask your groomer if she will offer you a discount for visiting midweek. Often times, professional groomers will give discounts to those clients who rebook frequently. Be sure to ask the next time you take your pet in for a pamper session!

- **Groom your dog at home.** Professional grooming costs for shampoo baths, nail trimmings, haircuts, and brushings can end up costing hundreds of dollars per year. Instead of handing your pet over to someone else, why not take on grooming duties yourself! Head to the pet store and pick up some nail clippers, shampoo, and fur trimmers and get to work! Use your own bathtub (making sure to place a towel at the bottom so your pet doesn't slip), a small plastic kiddie pool outside, or simply tether your dog to a tree and hose him down! While these items will cost a few bucks initially, grooming your pets at home will save considerable amounts of money over the course of the year. **ANNUAL SAVINGS: $300–$600.**

PET TOY SAVINGS

Spending top dollar on toys your pet might play with twice (or shred in five minutes if he's a large breed) might seem like a good idea at the pet store, but in reality it's quite unnecessary. Try these cost-saving tips to lower toy expenses for your furry friend:

- **Create a cheap chew toy for your teething puppy.** Soak an old washcloth in water, twist it into some sort of fun shape and leave it in the freezer. Give it to your pup fully frozen and when it thaws, simply repeat the process. This tip is best used for medium to large dogs as tiny ones can get too cold if they chew on frozen toys. **SAVINGS AMOUNT: $5–$10.**

- **Make your own dog toy out of towels.** Not only can dog toys be pretty expensive, but many are made from harmful materials such as vinyl and PVC which are toxic to us, our pets, and the environment. In the Colonial era, kids made their own dolls from rags. A canine version will make Fido just as happy as any designer plush toy. All you need to do is braid together three old dish towels. Before you start, cut two strips off the side of two of them then use these to tie the tops and bottoms of the braid together when finished. Easy, simple, and cheap! *SAVINGS AMOUNT: $5 FOR A NEW DOG TOY.*

WHO KNEW? QUICK TIP

A great household remedy for ear mites is to dissolve 1 teaspoon of baking soda in 1 cup of warm water and rub a cotton ball soaked in that mixture on your pet's ears. Of course, if you see a pet scratching his ears, you should always take him to the vet first, just to be sure.

Savings amount: $15 for medicine.

ROOM AND BOARD

One of the largest expenses that comes with pet ownership is boarding cost. Boarding your dog or cat can easily run anywhere from $25–$50 per night depending on the kennel location, whether or not it's cage-free, your animal's size, and whether specific care is needed. This makes any vacation a lot less affordable. Instead of resolving not to travel anywhere while your dog or cat is alive, try these money-saving ideas:

- **Hire a dog sitter.** Typically hiring a private pet sitter will be cheaper than boarding as these people don't come with the overhead of a doggie daycare service or large kennel. Pet sitters usually have the animals in their care stay at their own home and will ask that you provide the food, toys, and bedding for the duration of your pet's stay. Most sitters require meeting you and your pet prior to your vacation as to ensure that your animal will interact well with other pets in the sitter's home and to discuss any pet-specific restrictions.

- **Set up a pet-exchange with people you trust.** Seek out fellow friends or neighbors with pets and offer to watch their house/animals while they go away in exchange for them returning the favor when it's your turn to travel. Trading animal care with trustworthy friends is a great way to spend nothing on boarding costs, at the same time providing peace of mind that your furry loved one is in good hands. Likewise if your pet is already familiar with the people watching him and the environment in which he's being watched, he's less likely to develop anxiety while you're away. *SAVINGS AMOUNT: $25-$350 OR MORE DEPENDING ON LENGTH OF TRIP.*
- **When all else fails, take your pet with you!** Road trip vacations make it easier to bring Fluffy with you since you don't need to navigate airline

pet regulations. With an increasing number of pet-friendly hotels all over the country, there is no need to stress about sneaking your dog into the hotel room you reserved. Generally, pet-friendly hotels charge a one-time pet fee ranging from $25–$50—which is a lot less than multiple days in a kennel! Typically these sorts of animal-loving hotels will also provide food bowls, dog treats, and a designated "potty" area outside at no extra charge. Check out OfficalPetHotels.com or PetsWelcome.com for an easy way to search for those hotels, motels, or B&Bs that will happily accept your animals during your stay. **SAVINGS AMOUNT: $15–$325 OR MORE DEPENDING ON LENGTH OF YOUR STAY.**

WHO KNEW?   QUICK TIP

Sign up for free samples of all sorts of pet food and supplies by visiting All-Free-Samples.com or Hunt4Freebies.com.

DAY 20
FINANCIAL FITNESS PLAN
Set Up a Spending Fund

Today we look at a fundamental building block of any Financial Fitness Plan: setting up a spending fund. Getting your financial affairs in order and getting rid of debt is only as successful as your current spending plan. In this section we will explain the value of a spending fund and suggest a way to set something up that works for your budget.

1. What exactly is a "spending fund?" A spending fund is a way to manage your money by balancing your expenses with your actual income. A successful spending fund sets aside specific amounts of money in advance for pre-determined expenses. It's an invaluable way for people to get control of their money and their lives.

2. Define your monthly expenses as fixed or variable. Start by determining which expenses are the same every month (house payment, electric bill, insurance) and which change from month to month (food, clothing).

3. Create a new plan for all your variable expenses. Now that you can see where you are making choices with your money, you can start to make better ones. If your fixed and variable spending together exceed your monthly income, then something has to change. This is where you create your plan and take control: Estimate the amount you *want* to spend next month on clothes, food, entertainment, and other variable items.

4. Set up an account just for variable spending. Match it to your budget. This creates an unavoidable barrier to excessive spending. When your account is down to zero, you can't spend anymore! Overdraft fees are actually helpful in this circumstance because they provide added motivation for meeting your new budget.

DAY 21

GROW YOUR SAVINGS: GARDEN AND YARD

DAILY INSPIRATION

On Day 21, we look for savings in the areas outside of
your home: the garden and the yard. We'll first tackle
those big landscaping costs before moving on to a huge
money saver: the garden! You can save hundreds of
dollars in food costs *each year* just by growing some of
your own food. Then we learn how to handle the pests
that inevitably attack the garden and yard, and offer
frugal ideas for the pool and patio.

Today, remember that you deserve to be financially fit! And that means you need to set realistic goals. Just as when you begin a physical fitness regimen, you don't want to overdo it. Maybe you've experienced this situation: one month you pay way too much toward your credit card bill just to see a substantial balance drop, but you don't leave yourself enough money to live on and resort to using that very same credit card to get yourself through to the next paycheck. That's a common mistake. Even though you want to see results *yesterday*, be realistic and proud of the small steps you take every day toward financial fitness. This is a process of letting go of bad habits and replacing them with smarter, savvier ones. You won't necessarily see immediate results, but if you keep your eye on your goal, you *will* reach that finish line. Remember the fable of the tortoise and the hare? Slow and steady wins the race.

WHO KNEW? 　 QUICK TIP

French marigolds are not only beautiful; they're also the most practical plant you could have in your garden. Why? They have a strong odor that helps bewilder insects in search of their preferred eating plant. Plant some marigolds and your other plants will thank you!

DAILY SAVINGS SUBJECT
Grow Your Savings:
Garden and Yard

BIG SAVER: CUT DOWN ON LANDSCAPING COSTS

The largest yard-related expenses often fall under the category of landscaping. Here are some great ways to reduce costs on these biggies:

- **Buy 10 trees for $10.** If you've ever wanted to plant a tree in your yard, you were probably taken aback by the large price tag. But at ArborDay.org, you can become a member for only $10 and receive 10 flowering trees that will grow well where you live, plus discounts on future purchases. Their website is also a fantastic resource for learning how to care for your trees and troubleshooting tree problems. *SAVINGS AMOUNT: $40.*

- **Buy plants in bulk.** A flat of 12 flowers will almost always have a lower per-plant cost than buying a single plant, especially when sales and specials are factored in. If your yard can't accommodate a full flat, go in on one with relatives, friends, or neighbors!

- **Get free mulch.** Mulch is fantastic for your garden—it makes sure your plants are getting the proper amount of water while keeping away weeds, among other benefits—but it can be very costly. Save your plants and your wallet by getting free mulch from your community. Just Google "free mulch" (with quotation marks around it) along with your town or county's name to find out what free mulch is available near you. Towns, park districts, forest preserves, and other entities make mulch out of trees that have fallen down or have been trimmed. Just make sure to keep an eye out for weeds and other plant material while you're laying it down, and use only untreated wood pieces. It may be a little more work than store-bought mulch, but it's some serious savings! *SAVINGS AMOUNT: $100 OR MORE.*

Citronella candles are great for repelling insects, but they can be pricey. Get the same effect much more cheaply by mixing garlic with water and spraying it near all your outdoor light bulbs. As the bulbs heat up, the smell of garlic is released and keeps mosquitoes and other bugs away.

Savings amount: $5–$10.

MAKE YOUR SAVINGS GROW: START A GARDEN

If you don't already have a home garden, consider starting one! Just by growing some of your own food, you could save hundreds of dollars a year—not to mention that food you grow yourself often tastes so much better than what you find at the supermarket. When you find yourself with more tomatoes or string beans than you know what to do with, you can freeze or can them. Come winter, you'll be glad you did! To learn more about gardening, visit your local library or check out resources online. Growing interest in home food production has dramatically increased the amount of information available to those just getting started with gardening. Here are three ways to keep the costs down even further:

- **Use egg cartons as seed starters.** Don't buy cardboard "seed starters" from your garden store. Instead, use a cardboard egg carton, or toilet paper and paper towel tubes. The tubes will need to be cut in halves or fourths, then placed on a tray, while the egg carton can be used as is. Put a little soil in each, place in a warm, moist area (it doesn't even need to get any light), and wait for your seeds to sprout with some regular watering. *SAVINGS AMOUNT: $5-$10.*
- **Freeze your leftover seeds.** If you have more seeds than you can use this spring, store them in a sealed container in your freezer. The cold will keep them fresh until next year. *SAVINGS AMOUNT: $10-$15.*
- **Grow high-yield crops.** You'll save more money per square foot if you grow crops that are big producers, such as tomatoes, zucchini, lettuce, and squash. More bang for your buck!

WHO KNEW?   QUICK TIP

Use car wax to make sure your garden shears never rust. Just rub a little paste over the shears (including the hinge) to extend the life of your shears and prevent them from getting stuck.

Savings amount: $15-$20.

BE FRUGAL WITH FERTILIZER!

Many of the things you normally throw away can be used to nourish your lawn and garden. For example, did you know that eggshells help rose bushes grow? The shells offer lots of nutrients, especially if you crush them up and deposit them under the surface of the soil, near the bush's roots. The same applies to water that you've used to boil eggs in—when you're finished cooking, just dump the cooled, nutrient-enriched water on your rose-bush. Also, banana skins are excellent natural fertilizers, and the minerals they provide are not readily found in many synthetic fertilizers. Flat club soda is another great option for your garden. Try these other tips for a naturally beautiful backyard:

- **Use gelatin to help grass grow.** Have a bald spot on your lawn that doesn't seem to want to grow grass? Gelatin—yes, like the kind you make Jell-O with—can help! For a square foot of lawn, mix 25 packets of gelatin (about 6 ounces) and 2 table-spoons of grass seed in a bowl with enough cold water to reach the consistency of jelly. Pour onto the loosened topsoil in rows an inch apart and water regularly. The gelatin will keep seeds moist and it is full of nitrogen, which will help them grow. *SAVINGS AMOUNT: $30.*
- **Make your own bonemeal.** As you may know, bonemeal is an excellent source of nutrients for

your plants. But instead of buying a bag at your local gardening store, make your own! Bonemeal is just bones, after all. Save bones from chicken, turkey, steaks, and stews, then dry them out by roasting them in a 425°F oven for half an hour or microwaving them on high for 1–6 minutes (depending on how many bones you have). Place them in a plastic or paper bag and grind them up by hitting them with a hammer, then rolling them with a rolling pin. Mix the resulting powder into your soil for a life-producing treat for your plants. And you haven't spent a cent! **_SAVINGS AMOUNT: $8–$10 PER BAG._**

- **Fertilize with coffee grounds.** Coffee grounds are a great fertilizer for plants that need a lot of nitrogen, like carrots and tomatoes. But even if you're not a coffee drinker, you can get them for free! Many Starbucks give away used grounds as part of their "Grounds for Your Garden" program. Just ask at your local Starbucks. **_SAVINGS AMOUNT: $10 PER BAG OF FERTILIZER._**

- **Fertilize with epsom salts.** Epsom salts are one of the best natural lawn fertilizers around. They're composed of magnesium and sulfur, both of which are highly beneficial for grass. Magnesium kick-starts seed germination and is also a player in manufacturing chlorophyll, the substance that plants create from sunlight in order to feed themselves. Sulfur, meanwhile, also helps with chlorophyll as well, while simultaneously enhancing the effects of other fertilizer ingredients such as nitrogen, phosphorus, and potassium. It also deters certain pests such as ground worms. With all these benefits, it's no wonder that savvy lawn-care specialists have been using Epsom salts for years. You can either sprinkle them on your lawn using a spreader or make a liquid solution out of them by adding some water and putting the mixture in a spray bottle.

WHO KNEW? **QUICK TIP**

Is your hose full of holes? If you have an old hose you're no longer able to use (or an extra one lying around) repurpose it as a soaker hose. It's easy: Just poke holes along its length with a straight pen, then place in your garden to slowly water your plants.

Savings Amount: $15.

PEST CONTROL

You've planted a garden, and now it seems that all the pests in the neighborhood like it as much as you do. Keep them at bay with these money-saving suggestions. Chances are you won't have to buy a thing!

- **Kill ants with cornmeal.** Sprinkle cornmeal near anthills. The ants will eat it, but they can't digest it and will begin to die out.

- **Use a tennis ball to trap aphids.** Cover a tennis ball with petroleum jelly and leave it near the plants the aphids are eating. They'll be attracted to its bright color, and then will get stuck on its side.

- **Use garlic to keep beetles at bay.** Plant some garlic! If a head of garlic you have in your kitchen sprouts, simply plant it with the green part above ground.

- **Scare deer away with hand soap.** Deer are beautiful, but can be a huge nuisance in your garden. Using a vegetable peeler, peel slivers of soap off into your garden. Deer will smell the soap and think humans are nearby, and will find someone else's garden to invade.

- **Get rid of moles with olive oil.** Soak some old rags in olive oil, and then stuff them in all the holes you can find. Moles hate the smell and will stay away.

- **Use vinegar to keep rabbits away.** Keep them away with the help of some vinegar. First poke a few holes in a pill bottle, then soak 3–4 cotton balls with vinegar and place them inside. Bury them just under the soil and the smell will send them hopping in the opposite direction.

WHO KNEW?   QUICK TIP

Extra mouse pads can do a lot more than take up space in a desk drawer. Repurposed pads are perfect for extra knee support when you're kneeling in the garden.

Savings Amount: $8–$10.

POOL AND PATIO

You've taken care of your garden and lawn; now what about the rest of the yard? Keep the pool and patio furniture in great shape with these ideas:

- **Clean the pool with tennis balls.** Simply throw a couple of clean tennis balls into your pool, and their fabric will soak up oils on the surface of the water caused by bodies, sunscreen, and dirt. Take them out of the pool and clean them every few times you use the pool and it will stay clean all summer!

- **Limit your pump and filter usage.** Save money and electricity by running your pool pump and filter for the minimum amount of time necessary. Experiment by decreasing the amount of time you run it until you find the sweet spot. You should also set it to run during summer off-peak electricity times (morning and evening).
- **Repair a pool liner with duct tape.** It can be very costly to repair a torn pool liner. But duct tape can do the job. Simply cover the tear, and keep an eye on it to make sure it doesn't start to peel off. Believe it or not, a single piece of duct tape can usually last underwater for an entire summer.
- **Replace fancy furniture covers with bags.** No space to bring outdoor furniture inside in bad weather? Instead of buying pricey furniture covers, protect lawn chairs and tables by covering them with large plastic bags. *SAVINGS AMOUNT: $25–50 PER PIECE OF FURNITURE.*
- **Bring wicker furniture inside.** Before the first frost arrives, bring all of your wicker furniture inside to protect it from the cold. Freezing will cause the wicker to crack and split, which unfortunately, is impossible to repair.

DAY 21
FINANCIAL FITNESS PLAN
Paying Down Your Debt—
An Action Plan

Today's Financial Fitness Plan is a crucial one: establishing a plan of action. We've broken this process into three easy steps. First, you'll need to set a *realistic* goal for paying down your debt. Then, you'll prioritize and figure out which debts should be paid off first. Finally, you'll put your plan into action and carefully monitor your progress.

1. **Set an achievable goal.** You may want to be rid of your debts within a year, but depending on what you owe, that may not be a realistic goal. In order to come up with a plan you *can* stick with, you need to evaluate how much extra money you can dedicate each month to paying down your debt. A good amount to start with is 10 to 15 percent more than you paid last month. It may not feel like you're getting anywhere at first, but after a few months you'll start to gain momentum

and see results. Soon you might even find yourself willing to cut back even further on your expenses. (After all, we've given you so many great ways to do so!)

2. **Prioritize your debts.** Once you know how much you owe, it's time to sit down and analyze accounts. Which debts will affect your credit score the most? Which accounts have the highest interest rates or the highest balance-to-limit ratios? Here are some examples.

Five types of debt to pay down first:

- **Payday loans.** With mind-boggling interest rates, these sorts of loans should be at the very top of your to-pay list.

- **Accounts in collection.** These overdue accounts can have a terrible effect on your credit score, not to mention your peace of mind.

- **The IRS.** In addition to sending nasty letters, the IRS can garnish your wages, so make a point of paying off what you owe as soon as possible. If you need additional guidance on negotiating with the IRS, contact an accountant or lawyer.

- **Retail credit cards.** Often these store accounts have low spending limits, so it's easy to max out your card without spending much.

When applying for a loan, lenders look for low balance-to-limit ratios, so these types of cards could end up costing you in more ways than one.

- **High-balance/high-interest rate credit cards.** Credit cards that fall into this category can cost you hundreds (or more) each year in interest payments alone.

3. **Pay it down with the "snowflake plan."** Now you've faced up to what you owe and have your accounts in order of pay-down priority. Here's a tried-and-true method for getting to your goal as quickly as possible. It's called the "roll-down" or "snowflake" plan, and this is how it works: You use the money you save on your Money Diet every month to increase your payment on your highest-priority debt. When that debt is paid off, you use the money you save from having one less monthly payment to tackle the next high-interest debt, and so on, and so on. See how those extra "snow*flakes*" can quickly turn into powerful "snow*balls*"?

DAY 22

NIGHT ON THE TOWN SAVINGS TIPS

DAILY INSPIRATION

Today we'd like to address breaking free from "group think." It's easy to follow the crowd and mimic the spending patterns of your family, friends, and neighbors. If they're going out to fancy restaurants twice a week, then chances are you're right there next to them. There is comfort in this. But when you problem solve and take personal responsibility for your own financial choices, you open yourself up to making smart spending decisions that may or may not align with popular opinion.

If you need more incentive to ignore "group think," look at the findings of a 2011 survey by the National Foundation for Credit Counseling called the Consumer Financial Literacy Survey. It found that even in this tough economic environment where many are out of work, Americans spend more, save less, carry heaps of credit card debt, and did little more than worry about their lack of savings. Is this the trend that you want to follow? Thanks to the tips here, you have the wisdom you need to break free from the mistakes you see others making.

Resist the urge to go along with the crowd. In the end you'll get more satisfaction (and savings) from staying within your budget than you will from being just like everyone else.

DAILY SAVINGS SUBJECT
Night on the Town Savings Tips

In 2011, the average annual entertainment expenditure per US household was $2,572, marking a 2.7 percent rise from the previous year. As these costs are bound to increase in 2012, it's a good time to see where our expenses can be reduced. Small adjustments like seeing one less movie in the theater per month, cutting back on concerts, sporting events, and restaurant dining can save you an extra $150 a month with an annual savings of $1,800. That's certainly nothing to sneeze at! Below are more ideas for trimming recreational and dating costs.

RESTAURANT SAVERS:
HOW TO DINE RIGHT

Going out to eat with family or friends is one of the great American pastimes. Restaurants provide socially stimulating outlets for first dates, birthday parties, girls' night out and family mealtime. It's no wonder we spend so much of our weekly budget on the food-service industry! The following tips should help to curtail eating out, spending while preserving the experience:

- **Sign up on restaurant email lists to receive tons of freebies!** Check the website of your favorite restaurant to see what sort of incentive programs they offer for joining their email lists. Many offer all sorts of free food items or reward points just for signing up.
- **Go to TGIFridays.com.** Click on "Give Me More Stripes" to sign up, and get a coupon for a free appetizer or dessert immediately! You'll also get points toward free food every time you dine at there.
- **Go to Friendlys.com.** Friendly's restaurant offers a free three-scoop ice cream sundae just for joining their BFF program at Friendlys.com.
- **Check out IHOP.com.** Are pancakes your pleasure? Sign up at IHOP.com for their "Pancake Revolution" email list and you'll receive three free meals! You'll get one instantly for signing up, one for your birthday and a third on the one year anniversary of you joining the "revolution!" Not only are you racking up tons of free food items by joining various rewards programs at your favorite restaurants, but you're also accumulating points every time you order, which count toward additional free meals!

- **Visit EatDrinkDeals.com for information on all sorts of food deals.** Want to know where the Burger King free sample truck is going to stop? Interested in getting 10 percent off online orders from P.F. Chang's? Are you curious as to which fast food joints are giving away free food on Tax Day, how to get free coupons to Olive Garden, and when new deals are being released at restaurants? Look no further than EatDrinkDeals.com! They're a great all-in-one resource for restaurant coupons, sales, and other promotions. Sign up for their newsletter to have those deals sent right to you without having to search. While you're at it, sign up at Groupon.com and LivingSocial.com to find out about promotions in your area. Most Groupon restaurant deals allow you to pay about half the amount you would have paid. You'll never have to eat out full price again!

- **Get free meals and money back just for making restaurant reservations!** Sites such as OpenTable.com are not only convenient for making reservations at thousands of restaurants nation-wide, they also give you freebies! Earn points each time you make a reservation, then redeem them for a free meal at any of their partner restaurants! Another great site for getting money back on meals out is RewardsNetwork.com. They reward diner spending with points as well as with money back on your tab at restaurants nationwide!

- **Purchase restaurant gift certificates for less than a third of the price.** At Restaurant.com you can do just that by first entering your zip code or city. You'll be taken to a list of restaurants in your area that are offering $25 gift cards for only $10 or $50 gift cards for $20. Most of the big chains are absent, but if you've been looking for an excuse to try out a cool new local joint, this is a great resource. *SAVINGS AMOUNT: $15-$300.*

WHO KNEW?   QUICK TIP

Warehouse clubs like Costco offer discounted movie tickets purchased in bulk. For instance, Costco sells an AMC Gold Experience Movie Tickets 4-pack for $34.99 which is more than a 20 percent savings over buying them individually at the theater!

Savings amount: $15.

- **Take advantage of "restaurant week" for big savings.** Almost all big cities offer a "restaurant week" once or twice per year. During this week, you can dine at some of the nicest restaurants in town for the cost of eating at Applebee's! Most restaurants will offer a three-course fixed price, or "prix fixe" menu that allows you to choose from several different options for your lunch or dinner. Find a list of restaurant week specials in your area at OpenTable.com. This is an excellent opportunity to try that fancy restaurant you've read about or seen on TV but could never afford. Just make sure you stick to the prix fixe deals and don't order off-menu. That cup of coffee could cost you half of what you just paid for your entire meal! *SAVINGS AMOUNT: $10-$50.*

WHO KNEW?   QUICK TIP

Most museums offer opportunities for you to visit for free. If a museum gets money from the government, it's usually required to either offer free admission one day a week or to charge admission as a "suggested donation." Other museums have designated late hours that are free to visitors once a week or month.

Savings amount: $30 in ticket costs.

• **Seek out where and when your kids can eat for free.** No matter how hard we try, we always end up eating out way more than we'd like. It's easier to not feel bad about it when we go to a restaurant where the kids eat free. To find a bunch in your area, visit KidsMealDeals.com. Enter your zip code, and you'll find deals from chain restaurants and local joints alike; they even have apps for iPhones and Blackberrys in case you need it on-the-go! Remember, a restaurant that offers deals for kids also usually offers frugal prices for adult entrees so this site could potentially save you hundreds (or if you're as bad as us, thousands) per year. *Bon appetit!* **SAVINGS AMOUNT: $6 FOR EVERY KIDS MEAL.**

- **Eat at the bar.** As if you needed another excuse to sit at the bar, here's one more: many restaurants offer the same food at the bar as in the main restaurant, but for cheaper prices. You may have to order a few dishes to share since the portions may be smaller, but your savings will still be substantial. And since most restaurants also have table service in the bar area, you can take the kids. **SAVINGS AMOUNT: $5 OR MORE EACH MEAL.**

- **Forgo dinner at a nice restaurant for their breakfast or lunch menu.** First dates don't always need to be over dinner at your local super-chic eatery. Why not ask your special someone out to breakfast, brunch, or even lunch at the same place? Typically those menus are a lot more affordable than their $30-per-plate dinner counterparts. This way you still get to experience a great restaurant without putting yourself into debt for the rest of the month. If you still would rather take your date out in the evening, aim for hitting up those restaurants near you offering "happy hour" menus and pricing. **SAVINGS AMOUNT: $5-$20.**

WHO KNEW?   QUICK TIP

Get rid of babysitting costs on your next date night by arranging for a babysitting exchange with other couples you know and trust. Have a friend come over to watch your kids while you and your spouse hit the town. Even better, put your kids to bed first and then go out so your friend really only has to "couch sit." You may just be able to relax and let loose a bit more knowing you don't have to shell out an additional chunk of cash when date night comes to a close. The following week, head over to your friend's place to return the favor!

Savings amount: $20-$70.

- **Bring your own wine.** The easiest way to make dinner out an expensive one is to order a bottle (or two) of wine; but who can resist a little pinot with their pasta? Get rid of this extra expense by going to a BYO (Bring Your Own) restaurant which doesn't serve alcohol but will happily uncork (or de-cap) yours for you and pour it into a glass. Even restaurants that do serve alcohol will also often allow guests to bring their own anyway—just call ahead and ask before heading out. Some will charge you a "corkage fee," but it's usually a smidgen of what you would pay ordering off the wine list. If you'd only like one glass of wine with dinner, try asking if they offer a "house wine." Many restaurants will pour you whatever is left in a bottle from behind the bar for as little as $3. **SAVINGS AMOUNT: $3 OR MORE PER GLASS.**

LIGHTS, CAMERA, SAVE AT THE MOVIES!

As nice and convenient as it is to rent movies to watch in the comfort of your own home, there is something special about heading out to a theater to take in a film on the big screen. What isn't special, however, is the rising costs of movie tickets, theater parking, and movie concessions! Heading out to experience magic on the silver screen doesn't have to be a budget buster every time. Here are some great ways to reduce theater-going expenses:

- **See a movie for free.** Many museums, colleges, and even libraries offer free screenings of films throughout the year. Sure, they're not the latest big releases, but if you're in the mood for a film classic or an artsy flick, check and see if they are offered nearby. Many facilities even have full-sized screens in their auditoriums and they won't get angry if you sneak in your own candy! *SAVINGS AMOUNT: $12.50 PER TICKET.*

- **Get free tickets at FilmMetro.com!** These days it seems to cost a small fortune to take your family to the movies. At FilmMetro.com, however, you can score free tickets to advance screenings and movies that have just been released! Search by city or browse current listings for the options available in your area, then sign up and print your free passes! The pickings here are often slim, but the site gives you a sneak peek at future offerings so if you make it a habit to check back often, you may be able to snag free tickets to the latest blockbuster! *SAVINGS AMOUNT: $12.50 PER TICKET.*

- **Join movie theater and ticket reward clubs.** Join the "Red Carpet Rewards Club" at MovieTickets.com and earn points each time you purchase tickets through their website. MovieTickets.com will even give you 500 bonus points automatically just for signing up to be a club member. Sign up to become a member of the Regal Crown Club at RegMovies.com, which rewards you with one point for every dollar you spend on tickets as well as four points per dollar of concession purchases. Snag 50 points and earn yourself a free small popcorn. Rack up 150 points and you've scored yourself one free movie ticket! These credits will never expire, proving even more reason to join and reap the savings. *SAVINGS AMOUNT: $12.50 PER TICKET.*

WHO KNEW?   QUICK TIP

Game nights are not just for families and kids. Invite a bunch of friends to your place for a potluck poker night. If poker isn't your thing, host a "bring-your-own board game" night or a wine/beer tasting party. Skip the giant bar bill and entertain at home for laid back, inexpensive fun!

Savings amount: $40-$100.

DAY 22
FINANCIAL FITNESS PLAN
Combining Finances With a
Live-In Partner or Roommate

Whether it's a family member, a spouse, or a girl-friend/boyfriend, many of us have dealt with the complications of merging our finances with someone else's. The conflicts over how to spend joined incomes often stem from lack of communication, conflicting financial goals, and ill-defined partnerships. Today we ask you to consider some effective ways to reach harmony through compromise.

1. **The joint account.** Before you actually marry or move in with someone, decide in advance whether you want to get a joint account. Maybe you are comfortable with the idea of pooling your income, but you want an additional personal account for your own discretionary spending. Couples today have plenty of options for merging their finances, but it may take a lot of discussion and some trial and error before you find the one that is right for you.

2. **Mismatched spending habits.** You've moved in with your partner and have settled into a routine of domestic bliss when all of a sudden conflict arises over the new $200 piece of furniture you bought. You may think you scored an amazing deal on a must-have piece whereas your partner feels like the old one you were using previously was just fine. If this ever happens to you, today is the day to set a price limit for individual purchases. Talk with your partner and decide on a purchase amount that requires partner approval. For example, you may decide that any purchase over $100 requires the approval of your significant other. Once you agree on the same amount, both people must stick to the rule. If your spouse brings home an $80 beer-brewing kit the next day, you have to accept the purchase without any grumbling. If you see a beautiful $150 jacket at the store but you can't get your partner on the phone, you're going to have to walk slowly away. If you can stick to it, this pre-determined spending limit helps eliminate a lot of arguments. Give it a try!

3. **Schedule time to discuss your financial partnership.** Both you and your spouse, partner, or roommate need to have clear input on your budget. This can be achieved by scheduling a

specific time and date once a week to sit down for an hour or two and talk about your finances. Make today your financial "meeting of the minds." It's important to recognize that good spending comes from good communication. No matter how much money each person contributes to the communal fund/budget, both of your opinions and contributions should be valued. Establish and agree upon a discretionary money fund and make sure the money is accessible to both of you. Discuss investments you can make together that may lay the groundwork for a solid financial future.

WHO KNEW? **QUICK TIP**

Yard sales are great ways to make some extra cash that can easily be funneled into your entertainment fund. Clean out your clutter, post some signs around the neighborhood, advertise your yard sale on Craigslist.org, and walk away at the end of the day with enough money in your pocket for a fun night out!

DAY 23
KID-FRIENDLY MONEY SAVERS

DAILY INSPIRATION

The best things in life are free. Thankfully, for those of us on the Money Diet, spending time with our family and friends is the best choice we can make and it doesn't have to cost a single penny. No matter how much our life needs a Money Diet, we can always take stock of the free things that make us happy. We may think it's golf trips with the guys or expensive dinner dates with our husbands—but these are only valuable to us because they allow us to connect with the people we care about. We all deserve to indulge in those moments. We may relocate our weekly coffee date from the expensive coffee chain to the kitchen table, but we feel just as fulfilled. If you ever get frustrated with the sacrifices you make this month, repeat this mantra: *I don't need to give up the best things in my life in order to save money. Those things will always be there.*

DAILY SAVINGS SUBJECT
Kid-Friendly Money Savers

KIDS' EVENTS FOR CHEAP

Keeping kids busy is top priority for most parents. Especially those with young children. They can only run wild around the house for so long before everyone starts looking for something constructive to do. Before you pull out your hair, pay $10 per kid for an indoor play area, or buy tickets to the newest show or museum, consider the following:

- **Listen to cheap moms.** There are tons of websites out there designed by and for penny-pinching parents. FreeStuff4Kids.net is a great resource created by self-described "cheapskate mom" Randa Clay. It's a collection of links to interactive websites that your child will enjoy. Some lead to online giveaways of kid-related products, and others give you ideas for crafts and projects to enjoy at home. If you never want to buy a coloring book again, head over to Free-Coloring-Pages.com, where you can find printable images for kids to color, including those of popular cartoon characters. **SAVINGS AMOUNT: $10 ON INDOOR PLAYPLACE.**

- **Get a free circus ticket.** According to Ringling Bros. and Barnum & Bailey, "Parenthood brings many wonderful firsts—your baby's first tooth, your baby's first steps...and of course, your baby's first circus!" If you have a child who is under one year of age, sign up to get a free circus ticket that never expires! Just go to Ringling.com and click on "Special offers," where you'll find the "Baby's first circus" offer as well as other discount promotions. **SAVINGS AMOUNT: $27 FOR A TICKET.**

- **Go to free kids' workshops**. At The Home Depot's Kids Workshops, you and your child can build fun projects like toolboxes, fire trucks, mail organizers, birdhouses, and bug containers. The workshops are free, designed for kids 5–12, and occur the first Saturday of each month in all Home Depot stores. These fantastic classes not only give you a fun activity to share with your kid (adult participation is required), they teach safety and skills. In addition to the newly constructed project, each child receives a kid-sized "work" apron. Lowe's is another good source for DIY kids' projects. Bring the entire brood into any Lowe's store and build a free wooden project. Each participant also receives a free apron, goggles, a project-themed patch, and a certification of merit upon completion of the project. Clinics are offered every other Saturday from 10 a.m. to 11 a.m., and all building materials and tools are provided. Get the details at LowesBuildAndGrow.com. ***SAVINGS AMOUNT: $10 ON INDOOR PLAYPLACE.***

- **Go to free storytime.** Your local library is not the only place for storytime anymore. Bookstores big and small (like Barnes & Noble, for example) also host free storytime sessions for kids. Go to BarnesandNoble.com for specific times near you. Kid-oriented businesses like toy stores and clothing stores also offer free in-store story time events from time to time, so be on the lookout.

You can make a train toy out of shoe boxes! If you have a collection of shoeboxes you don't need, punch holes in the front and back and string them together to make a train. Make a knot on each side of the hole to keep the string in place. Let your kid decorate the outside like a train. Add some figurines as passengers and off they go!

Savings amount: $10 on a new toy.

TOYS YOU CAN MAKE

A Parenting.com online survey of 6,000 moms revealed that they intended to spend an average of $271 on Christmas gifts and toys. Go to any house with children in America at any time of the year and you will undoubtedly discover an over-abundance of toys. If you're a parent, chances are your house is filled with them. How can you keep your kids entertained without dropping insane amounts of money on new and exciting toys? It's simple: start making them. This saves your family heaps of money and teaches your kids the value of using their imagination and recycling (while curbing spoiled behavior).

- **Make your own roadways.** If you have young boys, you'll love this new use for old jeans: Cut off the legs and trim into strips about two inches wide and as long as the pants' entire leg. Turn the jeans strip over so the inner, grayish side is face-up. Have your child draw dotted yellow lines on them in paint, marker, or even crayon to make streets! Your kid will be so excited to drive their favorite little cars down them. **SAVINGS AMOUNT: $10 ON A NEW TOY.**

- **Make a dollhouse.** Tissue boxes and shoe boxes can be converted into a makeshift dollhouse. Cut off the tops and place three or four boxes together, cutting doorways between them once you've decided on the layout for your miniature home. Use real doll furniture, if you have it, along with pictures from magazines of household furniture, which you glue to the "walls." **SAVINGS AMOUNT: $25 OR MORE.**

- **Make high-fashion paper dolls.** If your fashionista loves playing with paper dolls but wants more outfits for a miniature runway, cut out clothes from fashion magazines. Remember to cut tabs as well so you can fold the clothes over the body. **SAVINGS AMOUNT: $10 ON A NEW TOY.**

- **Make a flip-flop into a stamp.** Lost a flip-flop? Might as well put the remaining shoe to good use. Trace a fun shape in the foam flop, then cut it out with an X-Acto knife. Now your kid has a brand-new stamp great for dipping in paints and ink! **SAVINGS AMOUNT: $10 ON A NEW TOY.**

- **Make boxes into blocks.** Make towers you can tumble without upsetting your downstairs neighbors! Cereal boxes can easily be converted into oversized blocks for undersized humans. Make sure to shake out any excess cereal and then tape shut the top with packing tape. Add shoeboxes to the collection, along with boxes from cookies, crackers, and even ice cream sandwiches, for a variety of sizes and shapes. You can cover with wrapping paper or magazine pages if you like, or use contact paper over the original packaging to infuse an Andy Warhol-inspired bit of pop art into playtime. Keep adding to the collection instead of the recycling bin. *SAVINGS AMOUNT: $10 ON A NEW TOY.*

WHO KNEW?   QUICK TIP

Museum passes are the most affordable way to immerse your kids in local art and culture without breaking the bank. You can buy an annual pass if you tend to go to the same museum a lot. You can also borrow your library's discounted museum passes. Some libraries even let you reserve them online!

Savings amount: $5 or more per person.

- **Make paper towel tubes into log cabins.** If you collect enough paper towel tubes you can make your own jumbo "Lincoln Logs." Separate half the tubes and cut out 1·1/2 inch squares at either end. Take the uncut rolls and stack them perpendicularly by sliding the end into the openings you cut. *SAVINGS AMOUNT: $10 ON A NEW TOY.*
- **Make a cardboard shape sorter.** Here's a simple toy to occupy your fussy baby for a good five minutes or so. On a strong piece of cardboard (you can always cut one side of a box) trace the circle at the end of a toilet paper tube four times then cut out the circles so they're just slightly bigger than the shape you traced. Your baby will enjoy pushing toilet paper tubes through the holes from one side to the other. *SAVINGS AMOUNT: $10 ON A NEW TOY.*
- **Make a soda can instrument.** Nothing gets toddlers out of rainy-day doldrums faster than sanctioned indoor noisiness. Get a parade going in no time by putting dried beans or rice into an empty soda can (a third full or even less will be more than adequate—you want a lot of space for the beans or rice to rattle around). Cover the top with tinfoil wrapped with a rubber band or else use masking tape to keep the filler inside. Now shake, shake, shake! *SAVINGS AMOUNT: $10 ON A NEW TOY.*

- **Turn food bottles into tub toys.** If you're looking for a cheap and practical toy for kids, thoroughly wash old ketchup, salad dressing, and shampoo bottles and let the kids use them to play in the swimming pool or bathtub. They're also a good way to wash shampoo out of hair at bathtime. *SAVINGS AMOUNT: $10 ON A NEW TUB TOY.*

- **Melt old crayons.** If your child has lots of little crayon pieces left over, turn them into a fun craft project that will give you some more use out of them! First, remove the paper, then place the pieces in a muffin tin. Heat at 250° until the crayons are melted (about 10–20 minutes), then remove from the oven and let cool. Your child will love the new, enormous crayons with unpredictable colors! *SAVINGS AMOUNT: $6 FOR A NEW BOX OF CRAYONS.*

- **Make some dryer lint dough.** Make a Play-Doh substitute for your kids with an unlikely ingredient: dryer lint! First save up 3 cups of dryer lint, then stick it into a pot with 2 cups water, 1 cup flour, 6–10 drops food coloring, and 1/2 teaspoon vegetable or canola oil. Cook, stirring constantly, over low heat until the mixture is smooth. Then pour onto a sheet of wax paper to cool. *SAVINGS AMOUNT: $5 ON NEW PLAY-DOH.*

- **Make cardboard swords.** Here's a quick, home-made toy that will keep your boys busy for hours, if not days: Take a large piece of corrugated cardboard and cut it in the shape of a sword (use two pieces and tape them together, if necessary). Wrap the handle with electrical tape and the "blade" with duct tape. Your kids can practice their fencing skills against each other, and since they're playing with cardboard, you won't have to worry about them getting hurt. *SAVINGS AMOUNT: $10 ON A NEW TOY.*

- **Make your own baby toy.** Here's a free, soft toy for your wee one: an old sock! Stuff it with old pantyhose, fiberfill, or even more old socks, then sew it shut to make a soft ball. If you're crafty, you can securely attach soft tabs of fabric of varying textures to the ball for added baby appeal. Sure, it might not look as impressive as the $10 ones you'd buy at a toy store, but your baby won't know the difference! *SAVINGS AMOUNT: $10 ON A NEW TOY.*

- **Build with cups.** If your young child likes build-ing toys but you don't want to pay for expensive blocks, buy plastic cups in several different colors and use those instead. They're extremely cheap and just as fun to knock down! *SAVINGS AMOUNT: $10 ON A NEW TOY.*

- **Swap out your toys.** When you notice your kids getting bored with a toy (and they always do), don't buy them a new one. Instead, stash the old toy away in a bag or box. Once you have several toys, swap with a friend for toys her kids have gotten sick of. Not only will you save money, you'll avoid the clutter that comes with continually purchasing new playthings for your kids. *SAVINGS AMOUNT: $10 ON A NEW TOY.*

WHO KNEW?   QUICK TIP

You don't have to have a pet to take your kids to the pet store! Most pet stores have plenty of live animals for kids to enjoy— not to mention all the doggie customers they may get to pet. Save money on zoo tickets and go to your local pet store!

Savings amount: $30 on zoo tickets.

DAY 23
FINANCIAL FITNESS PLAN
Teaching Your Kids
About Money

Today is a good day to teach your child everything *you* think they should know about money. Too often, parents neglect to discuss money with their kids at all—don't let that be you. Maybe there was a hard-earned lesson about finances that you never bothered to pass down to your older children. Maybe you just want to teach your toddler that four quarters equal a dollar! No matter how big or little the lesson, your kids could benefit from it (even if they don't appreciate it yet). No matter what age your children are, you are their earliest guide to financial fitness. Make sure the lessons you pass on are the ones that will steer them in the right direction.

START THEM EARLY

If your kids are old enough to ask you to buy them something, then they are old enough to talk about money. Here are some ways to introduce money to school-age kids:

- **Start giving an allowance.** Even little kids can learn about good and bad spending habits from a weekly earning system, as long as they understand the monetary value of coins and dollars. The rule of thumb these days is $1 for every year of your child's age. Kids can earn this allowance simply by being themselves or you can make it a reward system for household chores. Most kids need a little extra motivation to pick up toys, clean their room, mow the lawn, and anything else that is helpful to you and age appropriate. You can guide them in how to spend their allowance but ultimately let the choice be theirs. That way they can learn from their own mistakes.

- **Talk to your kids about commercials.** Young kids do not truly understand that toys and products advertised on TV can sometimes be misrepresented or sensationalized. They do not understand that companies create the commercials to make money. Teach them that they have to decide for themselves whether they truly like or need that product. Tell them to write down names of toys or items they see in commercials that they believe they "must have." If they really want these items, they will have to save their allowance and work toward that goal.

- **Look online.** If teaching doesn't come naturally for you, let the experts do it! Try these learning websites that are designed to teach kids basic economics in a fun way:
  - **ING's Planet Orange.** OrangeKids.com is designed for school-aged kids. It lets them journey into space to learn about earning money, investing, saving, and spending.
  - **EconKids at Rutgers.** (EconKids.Rutgers.edu) is a great resource for finding the best educational books about money.

DAY 24
DOLLAR-SAVING DECORATING TIPS

DAILY INSPIRATION

Just because you're reining in your spending doesn't mean your home has to look ragged. Even if your house needs an interior overhaul, we can help you do it without spending thousands, or even hundreds, of dollars!

Let's start this day by feeling good about what we spend our money on. Jonathan Swift said: "A wise man should have money in his head, but not in his heart." We could all use a little reminder of this from time to time. Today, let kindness be your guide. Maybe instead of buying a new pair of shoes, you make a donation to your favorite charity. Think about the companies you give most of your money to. Do any of them give back to the community? If not, today is as good a day as any to shift your spending to those companies that help the community and support your values. If you're going to spend the money anyway, why not do a little bit of good in the process?

DAILY SAVINGS SUBJECT
Dollar-Saving Decorating Tips

There's no need to sacrifice on your home décor just because you're on a budget. There are plenty of creative ways to brighten up a room, revive old accents, or easily make new adornments yourself, all on the cheap.

WHO KNEW?   QUICK TIP

Don't spend money on a no-slip mat for underneath your rug. Grab a caulking gun (or a friend who has one) and apply acrylic-latex caulk to the underside. Run the caulk in lines that run the width of the rug and are about six inches apart and it will never slip again!

Savings Amount: $50 for a no-slip mat.

BIG SAVER: REVIVE YOUR DÉCOR

Maybe your cushions are flat or the wood veneer on your table is coming off, but don't throw them out with the trash just yet! Revive them with these tips.

- **Fix flat cushions.** The beautiful cushions on your chairs are so flattened they're not much more than decoration at this point—now what? Let them sit in the sun for several hours (flipping halfway through) and they'll fluff back up! The sun's warmth is just enough heat to evaporate cushion-flattening moisture, but not enough to damage them (just don't leave them out so long that they fade!). *SAVINGS AMOUNT: AT LEAST $15 PER CUSHION.*

- **Try cleaning the carpet.** If you're thinking of putting in a new carpet, consider getting your old one professionally cleaned first. You'll be shocked at what a difference it makes, and you might change your mind about replacing what you have. If you still have stains that even a professional cleaning won't remove, a strategically placed rug or chair can hide them. *SAVINGS AMOUNT: $700 AND UP.*

- **Restore robust rugs.** To get the color back in your rug, pour 2 cups white vinegar, 2 gallons hot water, and 2 teaspoons ammonia into a small bucket. Mix well, dip a washcloth into it, and scrub away on the carpet. Soak up any excess with a dry towel. *SAVINGS AMOUNT: $35 FOR A RENTED CARPET CLEANER.*

- **Glue wood veneer.** Is the wood veneer on a piece of furniture peeling? Glue down the fragile surface with the use of a drinking straw. Flatten the straw, then dip the end in wood glue and slip it under the part that's peeling. Then gently blow into the other end to dispense a tiny amount of glue. This will keep you from having to pull up on the veneer any more than necessary while evenly spreading the glue underneath.

WHO KNEW?   QUICK TIP

The easiest way to freshen draperies is to place them in your dryer with a damp towel, on the delicate cycle, for one half hour. For extra freshness, hang them outside afterward if the weather allows.

- **Repair a braided rug.** If your braided rug is coming undone, it's not a goner yet. Try repairing it by using a hot glue gun. Just lay down some newspaper, then carefully apply a small amount of glue between the braids. Press them back together again and hold for a few seconds for the glue to dry. *SAVINGS AMOUNT: $792 FOR A 7 x 9 BRAIDED RUG.*

- **Bring back a treasured vase.** Just because there's a crack in your grandmother's old vase doesn't mean you can't use it for fresh flowers anymore. Just line it with one of those clear plastic bags you get in the produce section of your grocery store, and your problem is solved. It makes for simple cleaning as well! Just dump the water out, then throw away the bag with the dead flowers in it.

- **Spruce up old furniture.** If your furniture is weathered or out of style, that's not necessarily a reason to replace it. There are plenty of ways to spruce up old dressers, chairs, and tables. Everybody loves quilts, so why not drape one over that old chair that needs re-upholstering? You can also try using colorful fabrics on the fronts of nightstand and dresser drawers. Just get some scrap cloth from your last project or from a fabric store, and attach it to the dresser drawers with a staple gun. To have even more fun with it, we like to paint part of the piece and color-coordinate it with the cloth we're using.

- **Add new knobs or handles.** If your cabinets are getting old and worn, you can revive them just by replacing the knobs and handles. A good variety should be available at your local hardware store for just a few dollars each. They'll make your kitchen or bathroom look brand new!

- **Pantyhose and other nylons.** If your tights, knee-highs, or other nylon items have holes that can't be solved with the old clear nail polish trick, use them as extra stuffing in sagging throw pillows.
- **Raise the rod.** Who knew that windows appear larger—and will let a little more light into the room—when you raise the curtain rod just a few inches? You'll be surprised how much this improves the look and feel of any room.

MAKE IT YOURSELF

Décor and accent items can be pretty pricey. Fortunately, there are tons of decorations you can make yourself with items you already own. Here are a few of our favorite home décor crafts:

- **Make your own placemats.** We love these unique placemats for your kids: Buy an inexpensive or secondhand picture book, then pull out the pages and laminate them using laminating paper you can find at office supply or craft stores. They're water-proof, original, and cheaper than store-bought placemats. *SAVINGS AMOUNT: $12 FOR A SET OF FOUR PLACEMATS.*
- **Turn placemats into coasters.** Buying new place-mats doesn't mean having to get rid of the old ones. Cut them into several squares and use them as coasters! They'll protect your furniture in style,

and they're easy to clean! *SAVINGS AMOUNT: AT LEAST $10 FOR NEW COASTERS.*

- **Turn book jackets into art.** If the book jackets are always falling off your kids' books, you may be tempted to simply recycle them, even if it makes you wince a little when it comes to classics like *Goodnight Moon* and *The Little Prince*. Before you do, pick your kids' favorites, cut out the front covers, and frame them. Why buy artwork you think your kid will love when you own something you know they do? You can do the same for your own favorite books.

WHO KNEW? QUICK TIP

If you're into the shabby chic look, a chipped teacup or mug makes a pretty container for a small plant, herb, or candle. You can use tea lights for candles or fill with melted wax topped by a cotton wick. Attach the saucer to the bottom with superglue and you have an instant conversation piece as well.

- **Turn napkins into décor.** For an easy, inexpensive decoration that looks great in any room, frame cloth napkins. Use family heirlooms, or find some beautiful designs suitable for framing at stores like World Market, Pier 1, or Target. Place them in square frames and hang in a neat row.

- **Turn wine bottles into bookends.** A pair of wine bottles, either full or empty, makes a great set of bookends for your shelf—especially if there are cookbooks between them!

- **Light up a room for cheap.** If you have the interior decorating bug, but don't have much to spend on home accents, here's an easy way to add ambience: use Christmas lights. Great over a doorway, winding up the stem of a large house-plant, or draped across your patio, little white lights add a surprising touch of elegance. This is especially smart to implement in January, when all the holiday decorations are half off!

WHO KNEW?   QUICK TIP

Want to add a little style to your bathroom? Replace old, boring shower curtain rings with pretty ribbon that matches your curtain. Just run it through the grommets and tie a bow on top of the rod.

- **Make jar displays.** Have some beautiful clear jars but don't know what to do with them? Try putting photos inside! Add marbles, rocks, colored sand, or other decoration at the bottom then bend the photo ever-so-slightly so it fits the curve of the jar.
- **Make a vanity tray.** To turn an old picture frame into a lovely tray for your vanity, take out the glass and pry off the arm that allows it to sit on a shelf. Reinforce what is now the bottom of the tray with a piece of cardboard and a nice fabric of your choosing.
- **Make your own clock.** An easy way to add custom knick-knacks to your home is to buy clock mechanisms from your hardware store. These do-it-yourself clocks are just the hands and the motor, and allow you to add them to household items, turning them into clocks. Attach them to tins, plates, photos with a cardboard backing, or just about anything else in your home. All it takes is a little creativity!
- **Ditch the drapes.** Here's the thing about drapes: They're expensive, and a cheaper option is usually available. If you can sew, simply buy a nice, heavy piece of fabric, hem the sides and bottom, and cut Xs instead of holes on top. Run ribbon through the Xs and hang on a rod! Another

less-expensive option is a fabric shower curtain. The holes are already there, so just cut to size. Hem the bottom for a more finished look. **SAVINGS AMOUNT: $30 AND UP.**

- **Buy candles off season.** If you like decorating your home with candles, buy them on clearance at after-holiday sales. There's nothing wrong with burning a pumpkin-scented candle in spring or a Christmas-scented one in January. If that feels too weird, just stash the seasonal scents in the closet until next year's holidays come around. **SAVINGS AMOUNT: AT LEAST $5.**

- **Get art for cheap.** For beautiful art at cheap prices, try the gift shop of an art museum. They sell a wide variety of prints from their collection (and sometimes famous works as well) available in several different styles. Our favorite gift shop buy, however, is art postcards. Buy some cheap, black plastic frames (poster frames work well for this), pop your postcards inside, and you have a lovely mini art display for your wall. You can also buy an inexpensive art book and cut out the pages with prints that you like, or cut out the art from an old calendar, and frame the ones you like.

FLOWERS

Flowers are one of our favorite decorations, but they can be a total money drain! We've discovered lots of ways to extend the life of fresh flowers and get our money's worth.

- **Hairspray your flowers.** Who doesn't love a bouquet of flowers displayed in a vase? Unfortunately, it's not always easy to keep your display looking fresh and beautiful. To prevent flowers from wilting, gently spray the undersides of petals and leaves with a little bit of hairspray. It really works!

- **Keep flowers in the fridge.** Florists do it, so why not you? If you have room in your refrigerator, place your entire vase of flowers inside when you go to bed each night. The cooler temperature will preserve your flowers when you're not awake to enjoy them.

- **Decorate with fruit.** Instead of flowers, try fruit! Fill a large, glass bowl with citrus fruit for a bright centerpiece that's especially good for the dining room table. Use whatever is on sale—lemons, limes, oranges, or a mixture of them all.

- **Forgo the flower food.** Most powdered flower "food" works by lowering the pH level of the water, so that it's still good for fresh flowers but bad for any bacteria that may want to grow. You won't be surprised to hear, however, that we've come up with a cheaper way to lower the pH of your flowers' water: It's aspirin! Just crush a tablet or two into the water each time you change it and your flowers will last just as long. **SAVINGS AMOUNT: $13.**

WHO KNEW?   QUICK TIP

Extend the life of cut flowers with a little hydrogen peroxide. Just add a capful (3 percent solution works best) to the vase before you put the bouquet in it. The peroxide will keep bacteria away from the flowers' stems.

- **Keep flowers away from fruit.** When deciding where to place that beautiful bouquet you just brought home, steer clear of the fruit bowl. Ethylene gas given off by fruit will cause the flowers to die more quickly. Choose a spot farther away from any fruit, and your flowers will last longer.
- **Dry your flowers.** When bouquets wilt, remove flowers from the vase, cut off the bottom of the stems and lay them out to dry on the back porch. In a week, press various combinations of dried flowers between two sheets of wax paper. Iron on warm (not too hot) to seal the paper together.

Cut around the shape of the flowers, punch a hole and thread a ribbon to hang the creation in the window. In the fall the same project can be done with leaves your children collect in the yard. In any season you can use potpourri that has lost its smell.

- **Follow the garden rule.** If you're cutting flowers from your garden, do it first thing in the morning. Flowers have more moisture then and will last longer if cut early in the day.

DAY 24
FINANCIAL FITNESS PLAN
Explaining Your Budget
to Your Family and Friends

If people begin to notice changes in your spending habits lately, you may want to tell them about your Money Diet. It's not always comfortable to talk about finances with coworkers, friends, or even your own kids, but it's important to be proud of the small sacrifices you may already be making to plump up your savings account. Don't expect everyone to be on board with your changes, but they should all respect your goal to spend wisely and save more money.

Don't be ashamed to say you can't afford something, like lunches out every day or the annual family vacation (chances are someone else feels the same way). There's nothing wrong with recommending a more frugal alternative. Give friends and family time to adjust to your new perspective and you will hopefully get the support you need.

Being straightforward with your children is equally important: Telling them that you are trying to save money for the family teaches them an important lesson. It helps them learn self-control, good money habits, and may even motivate them to save their own dollars. Remember, you are doing this for your family, as well as for yourself.

DAY 25
THE GIFT OF SMART SPENDING

DAILY INSPIRATION

Now that your Money Diet is well underway, let's use Day 25 to look at ways to reduce gift-giving expenses. Here's a common situation: you go to the mall with a holiday budget in hand, but find a little extra thing for this person, and the perfect add-on for another person. Before you know it, the extras add up and soon the budget is blown and the credit card balance skyrockets. Gifts are a wonderful way to show our affection for our friends and loved ones, but they're not worth getting deeper into debt!

Today, take a minute to focus on the gifts in your life. Not just the physical things that surround you, but all the things that make you smile when times are tough. Try making a gratitude list. We know it sounds corny, but it really does work. Take out a piece of paper and write down 5-10 things that you're thankful for. Your list could include family members and close friends, your health, a good job, or even little things like a sunny day, a good meal, or a relaxing yoga class. You may discover that you have more to be grateful for than you thought!

DAILY SAVINGS SUBJECT
The Gift of Smart Spending

In today's Daily Savings, we tackle a delicate subject: gift-giving. We know this is a tricky one because you don't want to appear stingy when it comes to the people you love. Not everyone believes in limits when it comes to gifts, but we will show you how you can cut costs and still give a present you'll be proud of. From luxurious bath and body treatments, to deals on gift cards, and quick crafts, there's plenty to choose from! We even offer great money-saving tips for wrapping up your gifts!

WHO KNEW?   QUICK TIP

If you like to say what's on your mind, check out GlobalOpinionsPanel.com. Try out new products for free in return for telling them what you think! Global Opinions will even reward you with points you can exchange for gift cards for a variety of online retailers.

BATH AND BODY GIFTS

You can't go wrong with these one-of-a kind bath and body products. Don't be afraid to double or triple the recipe if you've got a lot of names on your list.

- **Homemade bath gels.** We love these incredible bath gels! In a medium bowl, pour in 1 envelope unflavored gelatin. Bring 3/4 cup water to a boil and pour it over the gelatin, stirring until it's fully dissolved. Then stir in 1/2 cup unscented liquid soap (we like Dr. Bronner's) and a few drops of your favorite essential oil. (During the holidays, try scenting them with seasonal oils for a special treat.) For an extra twist, add a drop or two of food coloring. Pour the mixture into small cosmetics jars and refrigerate until set. To use, place a tablespoon or so of the gel under running bathwater. *SAVINGS AMOUNT: $8.99.*

- **Bath bombs.** You've seen those fancy bath bombs in bath and body stores, right? Did you know you can easily make your own? You do need one hard-to-find ingredient, citric acid powder, which you can locate online or at some supermarkets in the canning section. (It's what reacts with the baking soda to make that fizzy sound—kind of like those baking soda and vinegar volcanoes you'd make as a child). This is a great winter craft because the bath bombs set up best on low-humidity days. Mix together 1/2 cup citric acid, 1 cup baking soda, and 3/4 cup cornstarch until you have a crumbly dough. Stir in the essential oil of your choice and the optional food coloring. Press the mixture firmly into the molds or ice cube trays, and then let dry for 24 hours. Remove carefully. Depending on the size of the bomb, you can use one or two per bath. *SAVINGS AMOUNT: $14.99.*

- **Cranberry lip balm.** For a seasonal solution to chapped winter lips, try this cranberry lip balm! In a microwave-safe bowl, mix together 1 tablespoon avocado or sweet almond oil, 10 fresh cranberries, 1 teaspoon honey, and 1 drop of vitamin E oil (from a capsule). Microwave on medium until the mixture begins to boil. Remove carefully as the bowl may be hot. Mash the berries with a fork and stir well to combine. After the mixture has cooled for 10 minutes, strain it into a small portable tin, making sure to remove all of the fruit pieces. Cool completely, and smile because you've made your own great-smelling lip balm!

- **Chocolate body butter.** What could be more decadent than chocolate body butter? Chocolate contains antioxidants that give skin a firmer, more youthful look. Place 1 cup coconut oil, 1/4 cup cocoa powder, 1/4 teaspoon vanilla powder, and the contents of 1 vitamin E capsule in a bowl. With a hand mixer, begin to beat on low. As the cocoa becomes incorporated, increase the speed until the mixture is the texture of whipped butter. Transfer to an airtight container, and store in a cool, dry place. **SAVINGS AMOUNT: $10.50.**

WHO KNEW?   QUICK TIP

If you're sending flowers for a special occasion, skip the national delivery services and websites. Instead, find a flower shop that is local to the recipient and call them directly. Most national services simply charge you a fee, then contact these very same stores themselves. **Savings amount: $10-$15 per order.**

GIFT CARDS

Gift cards have become prevalent these days because they're great for both giver and receiver. The recipient gets to choose exactly what he or she wants, and the buyer doesn't have to worry about choosing the wrong item. Plus, you control the amount you want to spend. If you have only $25 for a gift, you won't be tempted to go over budget. Also, gift cards purchased online often ship free so you'll be spared the cost of postage. Here are a few gift-card tips.

- **Liven up the purchase.** Some people don't like to give gift cards because they consider them dull or unimaginative, but it's not the case when you buy a gift card for something the person wouldn't normally buy for him- or herself. Stay away from the discount stores and think of places like spas, designer stores, and other luxurious treats. And don't think you have to break the budget here: even at an expensive store a $30 gift card might allow the recipient to put the money toward an item normally out of their reach.

- **Sell unused gift cards for cash.** Has that gift card to Smitty's Bird Bath Emporium that your aunt gave you been sitting on your desk for years? Head over to PlasticJungle.com or GiftCardRescue.com to get cash from unused gift cards! They'll pay you a portion of the total cost of your card (around 80–90 percent) and resell it on their site. Once you receive the cash, why not use it to buy someone else a gift card? *SAVINGS AMOUNT: 80–90 PERCENT.*

- **Get free gift cards.** Here are two of our favorite sites for earning free gift cards and other goodies.
    1. **RecycleBank.com.** Dedicated to helping the environment, this site rewards you with points for liking Earth-friendly

companies on Facebook, playing games, watching videos, and doing other green activities like pledging to recycle more. In return, you can exchange points for high-value coupons for gift cards to such places as Panera Bread, Walmart, Old Navy, iTunes, and more.

2. **SwagBucks.com.** "It's like a frequent flyer mile for using the web," SwagBucks.com says about their internet rewards program. Swag Bucks can be redeemed for gift cards from major retailers, along with many other items. To earn Swag Bucks, simply visit Search.SwagBucks.com and click on your point rewards when they pop up! You can also earn points by subscribing to their newsletter, following them on Facebook and Twitter, and taking surveys and polls.

• **Make your own gift card.** Create a stack of cards that the recipient can redeem whenever he or she wants. You can include things like babysitting someone's kids, watching someone's pets, or making a nice dinner for someone you care about. Be creative! *SAVINGS AMOUNT: $25.*

CRAFTY GIFTS

Be crafty, and consider making your own gifts, especially when it comes to presents for and from children. Save yourself the usual $25 gift purchase and make it more meaningful. But don't stop with our suggestions here: the web is full of more great resources on this subject!

- **DIY snow globe.** This is a good craft to make with children—and a great use for an old gift card! Take a small glass jar (a jam or salsa jar, for example), carefully wash it, and remove any labels. Take an old gift card, and trace the jar opening on it. Cut out the circle, and then glue a trinket—say, a plastic Santa—to the gift card, so that it will be hanging down in the jar. Allow to dry. Now add some glitter and water to the jar. Put hot glue around the edges of the gift card circle and insert in the jar, making sure to create a good seal. Then close tightly with the lid, and shake, shake, shake! *SAVINGS AMOUNT: $25.*

- **Give a kid's art calendar.** Looking for an easy, heartfelt (but inexpensive) holiday gift? How about a personalized calendar of your children's artwork? Pick up free calendars distributed by local companies, then paste drawings or paintings from the past year on top of each month's image. Your kids will feel proud of their work, and their grandparent, uncle, or godparent will love their new calendar.

- **Make a photo album for someone.** For the couple that has everything, why not show them how much they've already got? A tour of places they used to live (or go to school or work) is a personal and moving way to celebrate a special day. For an anniversary, find out where they met, where they had their first date, and where they got married. You can start out explaining each picture, but let the recipient take over. They'll likely enjoy telling stories as much as anything else you can give them.

GIFT WRAP

If you have a big family, or even if you just enjoy making gifts look extra-special, you know how much all of that wrapping paper, tissue, ribbons, boxes, and bows can cost. When you factor in holiday and birthdays and other occasions, you can easily hit triple digits—or more.

- **Wrap a present with a present.** Turn your gift packaging into part of the gift itself. For a bridal shower, wrap your gift with a pretty bath, kitchen, or tea towel. Write a recipe onto the gift tag, or use a recipe card *for* the tag, and tie on a bow with a beautiful ribbon. ***SAVINGS AMOUNT: $3.***

- **Use old calendar pages.** Use pages from an old or extra calendar (photo-side up, obviously) to wrap smaller gifts—two taped together are great for books or DVD sets at Christmastime.

- **Make sheet music wrapping paper.** Copied sheet music makes for unique and festive wrapping paper. At your local library it should be easy to enough to find books of whatever music suits your friend (classical, show tunes, rock music, etc.). Make a copy on colored paper if you can, and be sure the title of the piece shows when you fold it over the gift.

- **Make dollar bows.** Instead of doling out cash for fancy bows to decorate gifts, use your actual dollars to *make* the bows. Fold a dollar bill (or more, if you're a high roller) accordion-style and affix with a ribbon over a wrapped gift. As a variation, give a nod to Chinese New Year by putting two dollars inside a traditional red envelope and taping it to the top of a gift for good luck.

- **Wrap in kid art.** Have your kids draw on some taped-together printer paper and use it to wrap gifts that are "from them."

WHO KNEW? **QUICK TIP**

Do you have collections of paper napkins that are "too pretty to use"? Ever see them on sale? Take advantage of their beauty and use them as wrapping paper for small gifts or candy bars.

- **Iron old tissue paper.** Quickest buzz kill when wrapping presents: trying to reuse tired-out, wrinkled tissue paper and hoping the recipient won't take it personally. Turns out you can iron used tissue paper on low to get it to look "like new"! Amazing.
- **Save this year's stuff for next year.** After everyone's done opening their presents, don't forget to save bigger sheets of paper, bows, and pretty cards (to use for next year's gift tags). We keep our stash in one of those giant popcorn tins with a Christmas design from years ago!
- **Shop after the holidays.** You can get great sales on seasonal items that you can use next year. For example, the days after Halloween and

Christmas are great for stocking up on cheap wrapping paper and decorations.

- **Go green.** Here's an idea for your earthiest friends: wrap their gifts in brown paper grocery bags. Decorate a present with twine instead of ribbon and top it off with a simple pinecone bouquet! If you want to add a little extra personality, grab some markers or crayons and write a special message to the gift recipient.
- **Use a map.** Why buy wrapping paper when you have what you need in the glove compartment of your car? That road atlas you never use; the world map you never hung—give your old map a second life when you use it to wrap your next present. This is especially fun if the gift is travel or car-related. Add a compass or an air freshener to complete the effect.
- **Foil it.** Need just a little bit of wrapping paper but don't want to buy a whole new roll? Aluminum foil to the rescue! It's shiny and festive enough to add some holiday cheer without adding to your holiday spending.

DAY 25
FINANCIAL FITNESS PLAN
What to Do with a Windfall

In today's Financial Fitness Plan, we examine your spending habits and relationship to money by looking at financial windfalls (couldn't we all use one of those right now?). Every once in a lucky while, it happens: some unexpected money lands in your lap. It could be from a tax refund or Lotto winnings or from a relative who sends you a larger-than-usual check for your birthday. How you deal with this windfall—especially at a time when you're trying to pay down your debt—is essential to improving your immediate financial situation and avoiding the debt trap in the future. Let's look at three of the most common "windfall" scenarios more closely.

- **Tax refund.** A tax refund may feel like it's free money. It's not. It's income you worked hard for all year, but didn't get to see until you filed your tax returns. You wouldn't blow a whole paycheck (we hope!), so you shouldn't blow your whole refund either.

- **Bonus.** Some employers give out signing bonuses when you join the company or an annual bonus at Christmas. Don't get so used to the idea that this money will always be there or you might spend it frivolously. Companies can quickly rescind on many of these niceties (as we've seen during the recent financial crisis), so if you're lucky enough to get a bonus, don't take it for granted. Spend—or save—wisely.
- **Inheritance.** Your great aunt Bertha passed away; she wasn't rich, but she left you $1,500. Wouldn't she want you to go on a shopping spree at Bloomingdale's or get that flat-screen TV? Again, inheritances don't happen often, so think carefully before you spend, especially if you've got debt hanging over you.

We like to think of a windfall as a "nice" problem to have. The point is that you've received some extra cash, and it can help you achieve your goals faster—but only if you actually apply it to your debt. I'm sure you're thinking that we're complete spoilsports. We're not. You can enjoy *some* of the money as a reward for good work, but before it burns a hole in your pocket, sit down and think rationally about the best way to use it. After all, once you're financially fit, you'll have more money every month, not just this one.

DAY 26
BUDGET-FRIENDLY BOOKS AND MAGAZINES

DAILY INSPIRATION

We love Day 26 because it's all about entertainment!
Whether you love movies, television, or books, you'll
find innovative ways for cutting your monthly expenditures on all things media-related—without depriving
yourself. We start off by tackling one of the biggest
budget-busters: movies and television. Then we'll take
a look at your reading habits and offer tips to cut costs

on books, magazines, and newspapers. Finally, we'll give you lots of (legal!) places to get free music.

Today we look for inspiration from this quote from businessman and motivational speaker Nido Qubein: "Your present circumstances don't determine where you can go; they merely determine where you start." Most people struggle with their financial situation, so don't dwell on the things you can't control. Focus on all the ways you can save today by following these simple suggestions and move forward. You have a financially fit future ahead of you.

DAILY SAVINGS SUBJECT
Budget-Friendly Books and Magazines

It's time to cut costs on your reading materials and home entertainment collection. Luckily, new technologies offer more affordable options for doing just that. Read on for some of the latest ways to save on books, movies, and more.

WHO KNEW?   **QUICK TIP**

At Hulu.com, you can watch TV right on your monitor—for free! Play the most recent episodes of shows from FOX, NBC, Comedy Central, and other networks; or classics like *The Dick Van Dyke Show* and *Alfred Hitchcock Presents*. They even have a good selection of movies, whether you're looking for something to entertain the kids or a romantic comedy for date night.

Savings amount: $50–$75 per month for cable.

MOVIES AND TELEVISION

If you're like most people, your biggest entertainment costs fall into this category. Between the price of cable television, subscription services, DVD purchases, online rentals, and the box office, you can easily spend $100 a month—or more. To turn spending into savings, try these free or low-cost options instead:

- **Start a movie-lending circle.** Swap DVDs with friends or neighbors who also watch a lot of movies. You may want to choose a regular time to exchange the movie—for example, on Friday afternoons or at a weekly book club or school-related meeting. Movie-lending circles are a great way to discover movies you might not have picked out yourself, but really enjoy. *SAVINGS AMOUNT: $15–$20 PER DVD.*

- **Rent from Redbox.** Our favorite place to rent movies is through Redbox, which has kiosks at various stores for easy rental and return. Their rental prices are less than two dollars for DVDs—as long as you return them the next day. To find a Redbox location near you, visit RedBox.com. While you're there, make sure to sign up for email alerts so you can receive their occasional promo codes for free rentals! To get a free first-time rental, go to RedBox.com/movienight. *SAVINGS AMOUNT: $2–$3 PER RENTAL.*

- **Watch TV on your computer instead.** With today's online entertainment, you don't even need cable. One of our favorite places to watch TV online is TV.Yahoo.com/tv-shows-online because it carries the latest episodes of most of our favorite shows. Also make sure to check out ABC.com, CBS.com, and the websites of your other favorite channels to see if they broadcast new episodes of their shows the day after they air on TV. For movies, go to sites like Crackle.com. This site offers hundreds of free movies to watch online. They have an especially good collection of horror movies and comedy flicks, including lots of *Monty Python*. Also included are a few TV shows. *SAVINGS AMOUNT: $50-$75 PER MONTH FOR CABLE.*

WHO KNEW? QUICK TIP

To see movies for free before they've been released to the public, visit FilmMetro.com or Gofobo.com to see if they're screening films in a city near you. You may even be asked to give your opinion on a movie still in the final stages of production!

Savings amount: $10 (or more!) per ticket.

BOOKS

If you love to read, you know that books can be a relatively affordable form of entertainment. Compared with the cost of a movie, you get so many more hours of enjoyment. You may not realize that there are simple ways of reducing your current book costs. The most obvious way to save is to visit your local library instead of your local bookstore. Depending on how much of a bookworm you are, you could save hundreds of dollars a year—or more. Thanks to interlibrary loans, you can almost always get what you need. But don't stop there, try these other ideas you might not have thought of:

- **Get free e-books.** Download free e-books instantly at some local libraries and EbookPlanet.net. They have books across all categories—pets, business, finance, house and garden, computers, and even novels—all absolutely free. Other good places to look include Scribd.com, Free-Ebooks.net, and SmashWords.com. *SAVINGS AMOUNT: $10 OR MORE PER BOOK.*

- **Download free world classics.** When copyrights expire, the work in question goes into the public domain. That means you can get classic books for free, and it's all perfectly legal. Check out Project Gutenberg at Gutenberg.org, where you can download more than 30,000 e-books, including works by Mark Twain, Sir Arthur Conan

Doyle, Jane Austen, and other favorites, with more added every week. **SAVINGS AMOUNT: $3–$4 PER CLASSIC E-BOOK.**

- **Trade books online.** Check with your community's recycling center to see if they offer free books that people have thrown in their bin. Better yet, go to PaperbackSwap.com. Featured on the *Today Show* and in *Real Simple* and *Good Housekeeping*, the site allows you list books (not just paperbacks) you don't want any more. Once you send them to other users, you'll get credits you can use toward a new (to you) book of your own. **SAVINGS AMOUNT: $5–$10 PER BOOK.**
- **Get free racy romance stories.** Head over to RavenousRomance.com for a free, steamy short story each and every day! Then check out their great deals on full-length online novels. Another great place to find free online romance novels is PublicBookShelf.com.

WHO KNEW?   **QUICK TIP**

If you like to shop on Amazon, try Amazon Prime. For $79 a year, you get access to thousands of free e-books, free streaming movies, and a free digital subscription to the Wall Street Journal. Plus, you get discounts on shipping.

NEWSPAPERS AND MAGAZINES

Do you have three months of unread issues of *The New Yorker* piled up on your coffee table? Is the daily newspaper going right from your doorstep to the recycling bin? It's time to sit down and evaluate what you actually read. Gather up everything you subscribe to, and go through each item one by one, cancelling those subscriptions you haven't been keeping up with. Then total up your savings! Try these other money-saving tips.

- **Share a subscription with a friend.** The daily newspaper can get expensive. Often you pay by the week or month, so you don't see the costs adding up, but you are probably spending hundreds of dollars each year (especially if you have a daily newspaper subscription). Instead, find a close friend or neighbor and split the cost! Everyone gets a turn to read it. You could also do this with a magazine you both enjoy. *ANNUAL SAVINGS: $15-$180, DEPENDING ON WHAT YOU SUBSCRIBE TO.*

- **Go online for periodicals.** Before you subscribe to a magazine or newspaper, double check to make sure that you can't get the same content for free (or at least for less) on the publisher's website. It's also usually cheaper to buy a subscription online than to fill out that little order card that comes in the magazine. *SAVINGS AMOUNT: $10-$20.*

WHO KNEW?   QUICK TIP

Last.fm lets you create your own personalized radio station for free! Select your favorite songs and artists, and Last.fm will play other songs that are similar. It's a great way to discover new bands—and it's even better (and cheaper) than satellite radio.

Monthly savings: $12.95 for satellite radio.

MUSIC AND RADIO

Pretty much any computer these days comes with some kind of program to play MP3 and other music files, and MP3s files are easy to find on the internet. You should be aware, though, that many sites that offer free MP3s aren't legal, as there are laws in place to make sure that studios and artists get money for their songs. Here are some sites, however, where you can find free, legal MP3 files to download, as well as free, online radio stations tailored to your own tastes.

- **Get free MP3s at Amazon.com.** Amazon offers dozens of free MP3s as special promotions. You can also subscribe to an email newsletter that keeps you notified of new deals. **_SAVINGS AMOUNT: 99¢ OR MORE PER SONG._**

- **Listen to old radio shows online.** Try RadioLovers.com, which gives you free downloads of hundreds of classic programs, including *Amos & Andy*, Bing Crosby specials, and the *Benny Goodman Show*.
- **Keep an eye on iTunes.** If you use iTunes, check the store regularly for free tracks (especially before an album release date), which you can easily find on the main page or the music home page. *SAVINGS AMOUNT: 99¢ OR MORE PER SONG.*
- **Get free downloads at EMusic.com.** This site offers 40 free music downloads as an incentive to get you to join their site, which has more than 13 million offerings. Most downloads start at just 49¢ each, and you can sometimes get credit toward purchases just for joining the site. *SAVINGS AMOUNT: $40.*
- **Check out SideLoad.com.** For easy-to-download MP3s of all varieties, go to SideLoad.com, which pulls all free MP3s from a variety of sites. *SAVINGS AMOUNT: 99¢ OR MORE PER SONG.*
- **Subscribe to Pandora.** Pandora.com is nothing short of amazing. It's an online radio station that tailors what it plays to what you like, and it's amazingly accurate. Better yet, it will introduce

you to tons of artists you never knew existed. It streams the music from your web browser (you don't download any music files), and allows you to rate songs with a "thumbs up" or "thumbs down." For every song you rate "thumbs up," it will play more like it.

DAY 26
FINANCIAL FITNESS PLAN
How Much Money Should You Be Saving?

You've been doing a great job cutting costs and finding little-known ways to save, so in today's Financial Fitness Plan, you can prepare to create or build an existing emergency fund. The rule of thumb used to be that you should have three months' income saved for a rainy day, the idea being that it would take you that amount of time to find another job and get back on your feet. Now experts agree that, in today's job market, you're likely to spend anywhere from six to twelve months out of work and, therefore, your fund should be that big.

Does that sound like a lot? Don't be intimidated. Little savings every day will add up and you'll have more to contribute to your emergency fund. Here's where you should start putting your new Money Diet savings: If you owe money on accounts like payday loans, back taxes, accounts in collection, high-interest/high-balance credit cards—you should continue to focus every spare dollar toward eliminating that debt. In addition, the interest rates on these accounts are much higher than the small amount you'd earn from a savings account. But once you've started to get a handle on this bad debt, you can start putting your account further in the black. Here are some tips to get started:

- **Start small.** Put away at least $100 each month or 10 percent of your after-tax pay if you can.
- **Pay debts first.** If you're looking for bigger, faster results, apply the same "snowflake" method you read about in Day 21 to pay down your debt. Once you're nearly debt-free, why not put what you used to spend on bills into an emergency fund? After a few months, you'll really see the results.
- **Change your direct deposit preferences.** Arrange to have a portion of your paycheck deposited into a savings account—preferably one that's not directly linked to your checking account! That way, you won't be tempted to spend it.
- **Find out if your bank has a savings plan.** Many banks can deduct a certain amount each month from your account and transfer it to a savings account. That way, you treat it almost like a monthly bill that has to be paid—to yourself!

- **Keep the change.** Every time you get coins as change, put them in a piggy bank, and occasionally deposit these funds in your savings account. Your bank might be able to do a fancy electronic version of this, so that for every debit card or ATM purchase you make, they can round up to the next dollar, transferring the difference into savings.
- **Save a raise.** If you're lucky enough to get a raise at work, put the increase into a savings account every month.

DAY 27
SELL YOUR STUFF THE RIGHT WAY

DAILY INSPIRATION

An easy way to earn some money and clean out your house at the same time is to sell the stuff you don't want or need anymore. Did you know you can get money for things like CDs, sporting goods, and even ink cartridges? We'll teach you how to get the most money for your stuff, hassle-free.

Now is also a good time to think about your buying habits, and only buying what you can afford. Baseball player Earl Wilson had it right when he said that "people can be divided into three classes—the Haves, the Have-Nots, and the Have-Not-Paid-For-What-They-Haves." Your goal on the Money Diet is to avoid being in that last group. While you may feel like you deserve that new pair of earrings or that laptop computer on your credit card, it may not be worth the burden you now have in the form of interest and other fees. Using your credit card for items you can't afford to buy in cash is a surefire way to get into debt. If you have trouble resisting the siren call of your credit card, now may be a good time to cut it up and force yourself to spend wisely.

DAILY SAVINGS SUBJECT
Sell Your Stuff the Right Way

One person's trash is another person's treasure, right? So gather up all that stuff you haven't used in years and make back some of the money you spent on it! We'll help you learn where you can sell or trade items like books, CDs, clothing, furniture, electronics, and more! And we'll also teach you how to make the most of eBay.com and Craigslist.org.

WHO KNEW? **QUICK TIP**

When selling your used clothing, sell for the season! Most consignment, vintage, or other resale shops will only accept items that are appropriate for the season, so hold onto those used sandals until June!

BIG SAVER: SELL, SELL, SELL!

If you haven't used or worn an item for a year or more, it's time to get rid of it. But instead of throwing it away, let it earn you some money! Here are our favorite tips for how to sell or trade in your stuff.

- **Sell your books.** If you live near a used bookstore, stop in and ask whether they buy books. If not, check out ABEbooks.com, one of the largest marketplaces of used books online, and search for your book and see if it's worth a lot of money. You can also sell any book straight from the site! There are other places you can sell your books, too. Amazon.com has a whole section for used books.

- **Sell CDs and DVDs.** Sell CDs, DVDs, and video games online at SecondSpin.com, CashforCDs.com, and AbundaTrade.com. Look up the name of the product you're selling and they'll tell you what they'll pay and even let you print out free shipping labels!

- **Sell your old computer.** Go to Apple.com/recycling to find out if your old computer (Mac or PC) is worth something! If Apple can use the parts, they'll pay you in the form of an Apple gift card. You can also get 10 percent off an iPod by bring your old one into an Apple store. ***SAVINGS AMOUNT: $5–$853.***

- **Get cash for your gadgets.** Now you can keep your old electronics out of the landfill and possibly get some free cash in exchange! Services such as BuyMyTronics.com and Gazelle.com recycle or refurbish your old cast-offs and send you a check in return. Just fill out the easy forms on their websites. They'll make you an offer and if you accept they'll send you a box with postage to send your gizmo to them. They accept cameras, cell phones, MP3 players, game consoles, personal computers, and more. *SAVINGS AMOUNT: $5–$189*

WHO KNEW?   QUICK TIP

Don't bring your clothes to a consignment store in trash bags—if you think of the clothing as garbage than the store likely will too. Present your items like a boutique owner and the store might pay you like one.

- **Get money for ink cartridges.** Got empty cartridges for your printer, copier, or fax machine? TonerBuyer.com will buy them from you, and even pay the shipping! Fill out their online form to find out how much your cartridges are worth, then print out the prepaid mailing form and wait for your check in the mail. You can also bring empty printer cartridges into Staples stores, which will get you a $2 credit (up to 10 a month). *SAVINGS AMOUNT: $2 AND UP.*

- **Get cash or credit for clothing.** There are two options to get money for your clothing, aside from selling them online: a consignment shop or resale (vintage or modern) shop. At a consignment shop, you drop off your clothes and the shop will sell them for you, but you only get money when an item actually sells. At a resale shop, like Buffalo Exchange, which has outlets across the country, they'll give you money or store credit up front for your clothes that they think they can resell. Most resale shops will give you 50 percent of the amount they would sell the item for in store credit, or 35 percent in cash. So if the store thinks they can resell your garment for $20, you can either get $10 in store credit or $7 in cash. Make sure your items are clean and in good condition, and if you have any designer pieces let that be known.

- **Sell your used sporting goods.** OK, so you tried to get the kids into tennis, and it never worked. So instead of letting the racquets (and any other unused sports equipment) gather dust at the back of your closet, take them into Play It Again

Sports and get cash or store credit. (To find stores near you, visit PlayItAgainSports.com.) You can also try out UsedSports.com, which allows you to list your sporting equipment at any price you choose.

WHO KNEW? QUICK TIP

Get free packing supplies for your eBay sales at an upscale home store or gift shop. These stores often get products in good quality boxes with lots of bubble wrap.

Savings Amount: $4 and up per shipment.

EBAY FOR EXPERTS

Using eBay to sell your unwanted stuff is great, but there's no guarantee anyone will actually bid on it! Here are some tips on how to make the most money using eBay to sell your stuff.

- **Utilize your headline.** Your headline is the first thing people will see so make sure you're using it to its potential. Be sure to use all the essential keywords of your products including brand, model number, size, color, etc. If you have room, add in some words to attract people, like "rare," "antique," "unique," "stunning," or "one-of-a-kind."

- **Fill out item specifics.** eBay gives you a section to fill in called "Item Specifics," which is where you would list things like size, color, brand, etc. It's vital to fill out this section because eBay's search engines looks there for keyword matches. The search engines also look at your title and the first 100 words of your listing.

- **Develop your feedback score.** Many buyers check a seller's feedback score before buying from them. If you are new to selling on eBay it's important to build a high positive feedback score right away. An easy way to do this is to sell a few items in the beginning very cheaply at a fixed price, such as baseball cards for $1 each. When someone buys one, mail it quickly, leave positive feedback for the buyer, and politely ask them to do the same for you. You'll have a great feedback rating in no time!

WHO KNEW? QUICK TIP

Be honest—don't label something you're selling as "flawless" if it's not. You risk getting bad feedback from buyers and this will make it much harder to sell items in the future.

- **Keep customers happy.** It's important to keep up a good feedback rating so more and more people will buy from you. In order to keep your customers happy, make sure you answer all emails promptly, don't over-embellish your item, disclose any flaws your item has, package your item carefully and ship it quickly, and use PayPal as a payment option. Happy customers mean repeat customers!
- **Be aware of fees.** There are fees associated with selling on eBay and using PayPal. It's understandable that these fees exist; it's just important to know about them so you can price your item accordingly. The website EbCalc.com helps calculate the best price for your item based on all the fees.
- **Offer combined shipping discounts.** Make money faster by getting one customer to buy multiple items. To do this, you can advertise special combo offers, such as a shipping discount for buying more than one item. Plus, if you only have to ship one package, you'll save time and money too!
- **Be social.** Social media tools like Facebook, Twitter, Instagram, and Pinterest are great places to promote your eBay auctions! The more you publicize an auction, the more bidders you're likely to receive.

Nobody likes to spend a lot of time at the post office, so make shipping your items less of a pain by using the USPS or UPS websites. Visit Usps.com or Ups.com and all your shipping supplies will be mailed to you.

CAPITALIZE ON CRAIGSLIST

Craiglist is a great way to sell things locally and avoid the complication of shipping items. It's especially great for larger things like furniture because you can stipulate that the buyer must pick up and transport the item. The best thing about Craigslist? It's free to list items!

- **Get the details right.** When listing an item for sale on Craigslist.org, it's important to be specific. It will save you the hassle of having to answer a lot of emails with questions about the item, and it will increase the likelihood of your item popping up in someone's search. Try to use a lot of keywords that you think people might enter when searching for something. For example, if your item is a coffee table, list the brand or store where it was purchased, the exact dimensions, color, and material, how old it is, and if there are any imperfections.

- **Post lots of photos.** Posting photos of your item will dramatically increase the likelihood of it selling. Driving over to see a sale item takes a lot more effort than looking at pictures of it. Most people won't bother to see it in person unless they've seen a good photo of it. When you photograph your item, make sure it is clean and try to photograph it in a pleasing light and with all the pieces present. You're allowed to post more than one photo, so take shots from a few different angles.
- **Price it right.** If you're not sure how much your item is worth, do some quick research. Google your item and find out the current sales price and how much others have listed it for on eBay or Craigslist. You'll want to be somewhat in the range of your fellow sellers or you won't get any bites. If you can't find your exact item for sale, search for something similar. If your item is in poor condition, price it on the lower end of the range; if it's a fairly new purchase you can ask for more money.
- **Remember that Saturday is sell day!** Saturday morning is the best time to list your items for sale. It's the start of the weekend, when many people take time to search for and buy things. Post it as early as possible for maximum exposure.

Be wary of Craigslist scams and alternate forms of payment. If you're asking $100 for something, don't accept a trade unless it's for something you really need. Steer clear of anything but cash or a certified bank check.

- **Be ready to negotiate.** Unlike, eBay, Craigslist is made for bargaining. When you list your item, list it for about 20 percent more than you think it's worth. It's likely that interested buyers will offer you a lower price than you asked for, but if they don't, you just made an extra $10 or $20! And don't be insulted if someone offers you a lower price; think about it rationally and decide whether the offer's worth taking. If not, then make a counter offer somewhere between your price and the buyer's initial offer.

- **Don't get discouraged.** You will get a lot of responses from people who will not follow through. Don't take it personally and don't worry about it—that's just the nature of Craigslist. You should get a few people who do follow through and show up to see or buy items, and one is all you need! If you list something and don't get any buyers, you can relist it again in three days. Because it's free to list items, you can relist them as many times as you need until they sell. Someone will eventually take that unused blender off your hands!

- **Meet up.** If you feel uncomfortable with a stranger coming to your home to see or buy items, establish a meeting place where you can safely meet your potential buyer.

DAY 27
FINANCIAL FITNESS PLAN
What You Need to Know About Bankruptcy

WHAT IS BANKRUPTCY ALL ABOUT?

Bankruptcy may sound like a horrible thing, but for some people it's the best way to rescue themselves from a deep financial hole. Before you declare bankruptcy, you have to show that you tried to resolve your money problem. You are required to get credit counseling from a government-approved agency within 180 days before you file. If you do declare bankruptcy, you are legally declaring that you can't pay off all or some of your debts. This can free you from actually having to pay them. A court will ultimately determine to what degree you are responsible for paying back creditors.

WHAT KINDS OF BANKRUPTCY ARE THERE?

While we often hear about Chapter 11 on the financial pages, you will likely choose between Chapter 7 or Chapter 13 for personal bankruptcy. Chapter 7, or "straight bankruptcy," is the most extreme. You surrender your assets—yes, your home, too—to essentially wipe the slate clean on what you owe. It's a valid option for those with big debt and little income.

Chapter 13 provides a less drastic scenario. It temporarily stops creditors' demands of payment, buying you time to make deals over how much you will pay back within three to five years. Chapter 13 also requires additional education on financial management before filing.

DOES IT COST MONEY TO DECLARE BANKRUPTCY?

The irony of bankruptcy is that you have to pay to declare it—court fees, administrative fees, not to mention an attorney. The average cost of filing Chapter 7 with a lawyer is north of $1,200, plus more than $300 for the filing fee, says the National Bankruptcy Forum.

WHAT IS THE DOWNSIDE?

Despite its dire reputation, bankruptcy isn't a lifetime scarlet letter. But in the short term it creates plenty of obstacles. If you declare Chapter 7 bankruptcy, don't count on obtaining a line of credit for the next 10 years. Chapter 13 will affect your ability to obtain a line of credit for about 7 years. Your spouse's credit will also take a hit if you have any joint accounts.

It's also important to know that all debts do not disappear when you declare bankruptcy. You are still on the hook for divorce payouts like alimony and child support, student loans, and income taxes less than three years old. And if you want to keep your home or any other major assets, you must continue to make payments on them.

DAY 28
QUICK AND EASY MONEY-MAKERS

DAILY INSPIRATION

Welcome to your financially fit life! You started this book determined to make a change. You were smart enough to reach out for information to help you and we provided you with as much savings information as we could. Like any diet, the Money Diet doesn't happen overnight. It's a lifestyle adjustment, so give yourself more than these 28 days to start building new and better habits. We're proud of you for opening your mind to change and making a deep commitment to mindful spending. It's only a matter of time before things start to go your way and your account statements put you in a good mood instead of a bad one. When it does happen, be proud! Hang that savings account statement on the fridge and circle your savings in green marker. Every time you pass by, you'll be reminded of your success. Now you don't have to imagine all the ways that you can save and build your nest egg—you know them!

We'd like to leave you with one last lesson. It might be the most important group of tips in this whole book. Today's suggestions are money-making strategies. Sure, you have stopped spending every last penny you earn, but why not supplement your savings with a little extra income or some freebies you never knew about! It might be easier than you think.

SAVINGS SUBJECT
Quick and Easy Money-Makers

Don't stop now; you are almost at the finish line! Day 28 is about finding money in surprising places and earning it in unexpected ways. Maybe you have been searching for jobs and haven't had much luck. Change your strategy—you can be your own boss on the internet and get money for filling out questionnaires and rating products. Take control of your earnings and get some money flowing in!

WHO KNEW? QUICK TIP

You can get paid to be a website tester for UserTesting.com. They'll give you software to install on your computer that tracks your mouse's movements, and ask you to narrate a short video while you use the site. After answering a few questions, you'll be paid $10 per site you review. To find out more information, visit UserTesting.com/be-a-user-tester.

Savings amount: $10 per site.

FREEBIES

Chances are, you are qualified for some valuable free-bies, coupons, and services without even knowing it! Check out these possibilities:

- **Get free life insurance.** It's true: Mass Mutual offers free premiums for a life insurance policy with a $50,000 death benefit if you qualify. You must be between 19 and 42, be the parent or legal guardian of one or more children under the age of 18, and also meet specific financial criteria. For details call 1-800-272-2216 and ask to speak to a Mass Mutual agent.

- **Get government assistance.** The government has myriad programs offering financial assis-tance, awards, loan repayment, and other ben-efits. If you own your own business, are paying for college, or were in the military, are part of a minority group, or live in a rural area, check it out to see what you can get. The best way to see what is available is to go to GovBenefits.gov and fill out their simple questionnaire, which will give you a complete list of the programs for which you're eligible. You'll be amazed at what is available.

- **Go to HUD.gov.** If you've ever had a mort-gage insured by the department of Housing and Urban Development, you might be due a refund! Take a look at your paperwork or contact your mortgage company to find out whether you paid an upfront premium; then visit HUD.gov, search for "Refunds" in the keyword search bar, and click on the article entitled "Does HUD owe you a refund?" Then type your name and case number.

HIDDEN MONEY

We are convinced that there is money out there with your name on it! Try these websites to see if you can find some:

- **Find companies that owe you money.** Hundreds of lawsuits are settled every day, entitling purchasers of products to money they don't even know about. At TopClassActions.com, find easy-to-navigate lists of recent settlements and how to get money from them. During one recent visit, we found out Costco owed us a free three-month membership and anyone with AT&T internet service could get $2.90 for every month they had subscribed.

- **Find unused savings bonds.** Did you know that more than 25,000 mature savings bonds aren't cashed each year? To find out if there is a bond in your name that you didn't know or have forgotten about, check out TreasuryHunt.gov or call 1-800-722-2678.

There is over $24 billion worth of unclaimed property in the United States, and Unclaimed.org is the official government site to find out if any of it is yours. Search by name and state, and be connected to federal and state databases to see if there is any money, land, or possessions that have been left to you and are in government custody.

FREE COUPONS

Coupons aren't just for people who buy the Sunday paper! There is now an impressive array of coupon sites online that offer coupons on groceries, household items, toys, and more. Here are some of our favorites:

- **Get rebates on stuff you own.** Find loads of items on sale near you that are free after a mail-in rebate. Just visit PriceGrabber.com/home_rebates.php. This fantastic site lists hundreds of manufacturers' rebates and gives you everything you need to take advantage of them, including links to the rebate form online. Not enough rebates for you? You can also try Spoofee.com. Another easy way to find rebates is to check with the store's customer service counter.

- **Go to WhoKnewTips.com/extremecoupons.** Here we've compiled a list of links to more than 150 companies that offer free coupons on their sites. We've also listed a coupon matchup blog for just about every supermarket in America! That means you can find coupons that are matched up to what's on sale at your local store. Who knew finding coupons was so easy?

WHO KNEW? **QUICK TIP**

Before you click "complete order," look on RetailMeNot for instant promotion codes. RetailMeNot.com has thousands of codes at the ready to save you money on online purchases from retailers like Kohls.com, Amazon.com, and JC Penney online.

Savings amount: up to 30 percent off your purchase.

INSTANT JOBS AVAILABLE ONLINE

Whether you need a job or just want to make some extra cash, there are lots of ways to earn money without having to ace an interview. Simply fill out questionnaires, review products, or become your own boss using these valuable tips:

- **Make money off your style.** Are your friends always asking you for clothing recommendations? At StyleOwner.com you can set up your own virtual store from thousands of brands they have available. Send people to your store and if they buy something, you get 10 percent! It's a great way to make extra money without having to spend a cent in start-up costs.

- **Earn money by shopping.** Even if trolling the internet for coupons isn't your bag, there is still one site you definitely need to sign up at: FatWallet.com. Signing up at FatWallet is one of the best ways to start saving money online immediately and easily. All you have to do is log on to the site before making purchases at such websites as BabiesRUs.com, Payless shoes, Nordstrom.com, Buy.com, or Walmart. They'll give you money back on everything you buy—usually 2–8 percent, and let you know if there are any coupon codes for sales on the site. You can even earn cash back for using travel sites like Hotels.com, Expedia.com, or JetBlue.com, and if you use an online dating site, you can save a huge portion of your membership (Match.com gives you 30 percent back and Chemistry.com gives you 50 percent!). You'll usually have to wait several months for your money, but when it's as simple as clicking through, why not?

WHO KNEW? — QUICK TIP

Did you know that you can get paid to be an online juror? Many trial lawyers present their arguments to "mock juries" before their case appears before a judge. Just go to TrialJuries.com and click on "Sign up" to be included in their database of prospective mock jurors. If you're chosen, you'll be asked to review audio, pictures, and text evidence and answer a questionnaire.

Savings amount: $30.

- **Share your skills.** Do you have a skill others want to learn? Join SkillShare.com and connect with people across America who want to learn your skill, which could be anything from cooking to origami to selling real estate. SkillShare gives you a unique forum to list your class and your price per student, and will even help you find a place to hold your class. In return, it takes 15 percent of the fee you collect. A similar site is Limu.com.

- **Join a focus group.** Companies hire focus groups to try their products and share their opinions. Being in a focus group can get you free product samples, a bit of cash, and the opportunity for your voice to be heard!

Sign up to be part of a focus group at FGGlobal.com, where you enter information about yourself and then receive emails when there is focus group work available in your area. Or go to FindFocusGroups.com, which culls focus group opportunities from around the web that you can apply for directly. **SAVINGS AMOUNT: UP TO $200.**

- **Go mystery shopping.** Mystery shopping can get you free products and a bit of money on the side, but most of all it's downright fun. Visit a store, then fill out an online survey about your experience. The pay isn't much—usually not more than $15—but you'll be reimbursed for products as varied as designer sunglasses to lunch and a beer at a restaurant. If you're interested in mystery shopping, be careful of online scams. You should never have to pay to be a mystery shopper! Check out one of our favorite mystery shopping services, GAPbuster.com/mysteryshop, or search for mystery shopping and focus group opportunities near you at MysteryShop.org/shoppers, which is run by the Mystery Shopping Providers Association. **SAVINGS AMOUNT: $15 OR MORE.**

- **Take a survey.** The folks at SurveySpot.com not only want your opinion, they'll pay you for it.

Join for free and you'll receive 5–7 surveys each week to complete. For each completed survey, they'll pay you $2–$10 or enter you in a sweepstakes (or both!). This and other survey sites like MySurvey.com, EPoll.com, and Toluna.com can take time to maneuver, but they're a great way to earn some extra cash while you're messing around on the web. *SAVINGS AMOUNT: $2–$10*

WHO KNEW?   QUICK TIP

Zilok.com allows you to make money by renting out your car, vacation home, tools, camera, lawn mower, TV, video game console, and more. (Unfortunately, you can't rent out your kids.) For more information, go to US.Zilok.com/support.

- **Make money off your extra space.** Renting out a spare room has long been a way for families to make ends meet in tough times. But even if you don't want someone else living in your home, you may be able to rent out storage space in your garage. If you live near a train station or in a densely populated area, you may also want to think about renting out your driveway for a parking space. Place an ad on Craigslist.org or in your local paper and see if you get any bites.

- **Sell your music or photos on GumRoad.com.** In this day and age, many of the things entrepreneurs sell come in the form of files—whether they're songs, photography, ebooks, designs, or any of the other many things that fill our online world. GumRoad.com makes it ridiculously easy to sell files to friends, family, and anyone who follows you online. Simply upload a file and set your price, and GumRoad gives you a link you can email, Tweet, or share on Facebook. To buy, all someone has to do is enter their email and credit card info, and GumRoad sends them an email with a link to your content! Best of all, Gum-Road's cut is only 25¢ plus 5 percent, lower than most other sites that allow you to sell products.

- **Open an Etsy shop.** At Etsy.com, you will find millions of gorgeous handcrafted items for sale. If you are good at making anything (knitted hats, collages, jewelry, candles, etc.), you can easily sell your items online to a vast audience by opening your own Etsy "Shop." It's free to set up your shop, but it does cost 20¢ to list an item. That being said, if you list a $15 knitted hat for 20¢ and someone buys it, you've made $14.80! Etsy charges only 3.5 percent in transaction fees for each sale so you can enjoy just about all of your profits.

FLEXIBLE SECOND JOBS

If you're really struggling with your current income or you just want to be your own boss for a change, consider these job ideas. They're flexible in terms of where and when you can work, so they mesh more easily with a nine to five job.

- **Become a tutor.** If you know how to play an instrument or have a background in math, science, or English, tutoring may be a good way to make some extra cash. Put up fliers in your area, post an ad on Craigslist.org, and talk to local schools and after-school programs to see if they have children in need of tutoring. Make sure to have your résumé handy, and provide references, even if they're in the form of your friends whose children you have taught a skill. If you have a bachelor's degree and a fast internet connection, you can also sign up to be a tutor at EduWizards.com.

- **Go pro with your baking.** If your cookies, cakes, pies, brownies, or other sweets always get rave reviews, consider putting your skills to work selling baked goods. Visit local coffee shops, delis, and independently owned restaurants with some of your creations in hand and see if they would be willing to give you a cut of any sales or purchase them outright. For those who love to bake, this could be an easy way to turn your hobby into some cash.

- **Work with animals.** No matter what shape the economy is in, people will always need dog-walkers and cat-sitters. Both jobs can get you $10–$20 an hour, and you'll get to spend time with some furry friends (who will never drink the last of the coffee in the office kitchen-ette). The trick to this business is to get a lot of clients in close proximity to each other, so you don't have to spend a lot of time and money on travel. Try advertising at pet stores, groomers', and veterinary offices near you. Just make sure to check out licensing and insurance require-ments in your state.

WHO KNEW?   QUICK TIP

You can make money by starting a call center in your home when you sign up at AlpineAccess.com or Arise.com/work-at-home. You could make up to $14 an hour and won't even have to change out of your pajamas.

DAY 28
FINANCIAL FITNESS
Investment 101

Many people think that investing is only for those who have a lot of extra money lying around. Not true. There are plenty of ways to invest small sums of money from your paycheck in a way that helps you grow a substantial lump sum for the future. Here are some notable ways to do that:

RETIREMENT

- **Use your company's 401K plan.** If your company offers a 401K program (especially if they do any matching), the first step in your financial plan should be to enroll. Take advantage of this income-tax free investment and you can safely build toward your retirement savings.
- **Put money in a Roth or Traditional IRA.** Find out if you qualify for the Roth IRA. If not, put money in a Traditional IRA. These investment accounts let you sock money away for retirement while offering significant tax benefits.

INVESTING IN THE STOCK MARKET

If you want to venture beyond the 401K account, then maybe it's time to invest in the stock market. Find a brokerage firm you like and give yourself a chance to make more money on a portion of your savings. If you don't already know the basics, here are answers to a few common questions:

What is the difference between stocks, bonds, and mutual funds?

Stocks allow you to buy a small piece of a company, and they reward you if the value of that company increases. Bonds allow you to loan your money to a company or government for a set period of time for an agreed-upon interest rate. Mutual funds are different because they pool money from many different investors and buy a group of stocks and bonds. This serves to lower the risk of investing.

How much do I need to start investing in stocks and mutual funds?

Every broker has their own minimum opening balance requirement and may charge maintenance fees if your balance goes below a set amount. To open an account, most firms require at least $1,000.

How do you decide what firm and what kind of broker you need?

For those who are new to investing, it may be best to avoid discount brokers and sign on with a full-service or traditional brokerage firm instead. That way, you'll have the advice of a personal stock broker to guide you in your investments and to explain how your investments are faring over time. That being said, websites like ETrade.com are blurring the line between the two. Like more and more online trading sites, they offer live help and guidance from professionals. Compare transaction costs between brokerage firms and get recommendations from friends before you decide who you want to work with.

INDEX